Pearls of Wisdom
佛光祈願文 (2)

Prayers for Engaged Living II

Professions and Society
社會‧職業

Buddhism and Dharma Service
佛教‧法會

By Venerable Master Hsing Yun

Translated by Shujan Cheng and Tom Manzo

© 2003 Buddha's Light Publishing

By Venerable Master Hsing Yun
Translated by Shujan Cheng and Tom Manzo
Edited by James Baquet, Pey-Rong Lee, and Brenda Bolinger
Book and cover designed by Carol Peng, Mei-Chi Shih, and Ching Tay

Published by Buddha's Light Publishing
3456 S. Glenmark Drive
Hacienda Heights, CA 91745, U.S.A.
Tel: (626) 923-5143   Fax: (626) 923-5145
E-mail: itc@blia.org

Protected by copyright under the terms of the International Copyright Union; all rights reserved. Except for fair use in book reviews, no part of this book may be reproduced for any reason by any means, including any method of photographic reproduction, without permission of the publisher.

Printed in Taiwan.

ISBN 0-9717495-6-6
Library of Congress Control Number 2003103867

Contents 《目錄》

Foreword 前言	i
Preface 序	iii
Introduction 本書介紹	ix
Acknowledgments 感謝	x
A Prayer for Our Armed Forces 為三軍將士祈願文	1
A Prayer for Explorers 為探險者祈願文	5
A Prayer for Sanitation Workers 為清道夫祈願文	9
A Prayer for Farmers, Fishery Workers, and Laborers 為農漁勞工祈願文	13
A Prayer for Health-Care Professionals 為醫護人員祈願文	17
A Prayer for Police Officers 為警察祈願文	21
A Prayer for Our Volunteers 為義工祈願文	25
A Prayer for Construction Professionals 為工程人員祈願文	29
A Prayer for Emergency Rescue and Relief Workers 為救難人員祈願文	33
A Prayer for Firefighters 為消防人員祈願文	37
A Prayer for Performing Artists 為演藝人員祈願文	40
A Prayer for Transportation Industry Professionals 為交通人員祈願文	44

A Prayer for Maritime Professionals 為海域工作者祈願文	48
A Prayer for Prostitutes 為煙花女子祈願文	52
A Prayer for the Drivers of All Vehicles 為汽車駕駛祈願文	56
A Prayer for Our Teachers 為教師祈願文	60
A Prayer for Mass Communication Professionals 為大眾傳播者祈願文	64
A Prayer for Postal and Cable Service Professionals 為郵電人員祈願文	68
A Prayer for Recycling Professionals 為資源回收者祈願文	72
A Prayer in Honor of Servicepeople Killed in Action 為陣亡將士祈願文	76
A Prayer for Blessings on Our Nation 為國家祈福祈願文	80
A Prayer for World Peace 為世界和平祈願文	83
A Prayer for Our Natural Environment 為自然生態祈願文	87
A Prayer for People of All Vocations and Endeavors 為社會大眾祈願文	91
A Prayer for Victims and Families of the September 11th Disaster 為九一一罹難者祈願文	95
A Prayer To Respectfully Welcome a Relic of the Buddha's Tooth 恭迎佛牙祈願文	99
A Prayer for the Buddha's Birthday 佛誕節祈願文	103

A Prayer for the Consecration of
a Newly-Completed Statue of Buddha　*107*
　佛像開光祈願文

A Prayer for Taking Refuge in the Triple Gem　*111*
　皈依三寶祈願文

A Prayer for Receiving and Upholding
the Five Precepts　*115*
　受持五戒祈願文

A Prayer for the Offering of Light　*119*
　獻燈祈願文

A Prayer for Those Who Are Becoming
Monastics　*123*
　為出家修道者祈願文

A Prayer for Devotees　*127*
　為在家信眾祈願文

A Prayer for People Who Build and
Support Schools　*132*
　為興學功德主祈願文

A Prayer for a Buddhist Wedding Ceremony　*136*
　佛化婚禮祈願文

A Prayer for the Dharma Propagators　*140*
　為弘法善知識祈願文

A Prayer for a Visitation to a Buddhist Family　*145*
　家庭普照祈願文

A Prayer for the People Who Listen to the Dharma　*149*
　為聽經聞法者祈願文

A Prayer for Parents of Monastics　*153*
　出家眾為父母祈願文

A Prayer for Children Who Are Monastics　*157*
　為出家兒女祈願文

A Prayer for the Dharma Service　*162*
　共修法會祈願文

A Prayer to Amitabha Buddha　*166*
　向阿彌陀佛祈願文

A Prayer to the Medicine Buddha　*170*
　向藥師如來祈願文

A Prayer to Avalokitesvara Bodhisattva 向觀世音菩薩祈願文	*174*
A Prayer for Devoir Chanting in Three Periods 為三時繫念祈願文	*178*
A Prayer for the Repentance Service of Emperor Liang 梁皇寶懺祈願文	*182*
A Prayer for the Repentance Service of Compassionate Samadhi Water 慈悲三昧水懺祈願文	*186*
A Prayer for the Yogacara Dharma Service 燄口祈願文	*190*
A Prayer for Pilgrimage 朝山祈願文	*195*
A Prayer for Deities and Ghosts 為神鬼靈祇祈願文	*199*
Endnotes and Glossary 註解與名相解說	*203*

Foreword

Of all the religions in the world, Buddhism appears to be the one that is most blessed with teachings that clearly explain the human condition with all its foibles and grandeur. We need not look past the founder of the religion, Siddartha Gautama, the Buddha, as one who eventually lived a life that was faultless in behavior and motivation after living a life of self-indulgence. The mendicant organization he founded at the inception of his teaching career for the benefit of those who wished to follow the prescribed spiritual path set forth by the Buddha was not intended to lead its practitioners to the delights of heaven or to experience fruitful and happy rebirths. Rather, it set forth a regimen designed to end the imperfections and anxieties of this life.

As successful as the regimen was in bringing about the transformation of seekers, Buddhism, as it developed over the centuries within India and beyond, became identified with other practices that in some instances had little or nothing to do with the path laid out by the Buddha. Different needs of the Buddhist community arose and changing cultural proclivities of the wider societies manifested themselves, both leading to Buddhist communities that often bear little resemblance to the founder's own vision of his community. This is not generally recognized by the non-discerning members—whether leaders or their followers—within the religious tradition. There are, nonetheless, throughout the history of any religious movement those gifted and insightful few who possess the vision to recognize the purpose and true teaching of the religion and take steps to restore it to its proper task. Very often, such a vision is misunderstood, attacked, or ignored. A religious movement having a founder or a recognizable historical beginning, succeeds, in the opinion of many practitioners and scholars of religion, only if its teachings are maintained and interpreted according to the perceived original intent of the founder or early leaders.

Precious are those teachers and visionaries who remind us

of the original intent of the founder and pioneers of the religion. They do not take on a simple mission, for it is easier to tell the people what they wish to hear. In Buddhism, one such teacher is Grand Master Hsing Yun, the founder of one of the most successful Buddhist movements in Taiwan, Fo Guang Shan. The Grand Master espouses "Humanistic Buddhism," a form of Buddhism that may give the impression to some that it is a sectarian or deviant movement bearing little resemblance to the Buddha's teachings. Yet, labels can be deceiving. "Humanistic" has little to do with the philosophy of humanism as it has developed in the West. A superficial resemblance between Western humanism and Humanistic Buddhism does exist, but the latter merely stresses the simple but sometimes forgotten fact that Buddhism is for humans and that certain human qualities should be activated: compassion, ethical responsibility, and wisdom. Furthermore, Humanistic Buddhism does not stress so much the afterlife as it does the here and now, and all those relationships and obligations incumbent upon individuals within the framework of family, community, nation, the world, and the environment. *Pearls of Wisdom* illustrates this emphasis, and it teaches how one may nurture those emotions, motivations, and acts that portray a balanced, ethical, compassionate, informed, and responsible life for the benefit of humanity.

James A. Santucci
Department of Comparative Religion
California State University
Fullerton, California, USA

Preface

Sixty years ago, in the spring of 1939, I shaved my head and joined a monastery in Qixia Shan. I was twelve years old. Late in the quiet night I would often kneel in the Buddha Hall to pray to Buddha and Avalokitesvara Bodhisattva for intelligence and wisdom, and for blessings, protection, and help. I felt that this cultivation through prayer increased my own strength and enhanced my own faith. Therefore, for the past sixty years, prayer has always been an essential part of my daily cultivation as a monastic.

Prayer is originally embodied in the ceremony of all religions. When I was young, in the old monastery there were formal prayers on the first and fifteenth of each month. However, those prayers were long, and their profound meaning was very difficult for beginners to comprehend. Thus, I myself could only follow the instructions of the teachers to pray in the morning and evening as follows: "We all vow to initiate the bodhi mind... lotus flowers grow everywhere... your disciples' minds are confused... we pay respect to Avalokitesvara Bodhisattva for intelligence, wisdom..." From that moment on, I made a vow in my mind to compose a set of prayers for the general use of the whole of Buddhism as well as for the masses of society.

For many years, I always tried to pray for the people directly involved in the majestic Buddhist ceremonies and in the ceremonies for happy occasions, funeral and wedding celebrations, and Buddhist family meetings. In the past, the document-like prayers to the Buddha that were read in public in Mainland China, as well as the report-like prayers in Taiwan, all required a certain cadence to recite them correctly. They could not be recited by the general public. To make the prayers more accessible, I adapted them into plain-spoken-language prayers and was pleased by their effect. Later on, Fo Guang disciples all over the world began to copy the prayers for use in all kinds of gatherings. All of them said the prayers moved them deeply.

Buddhist hymns and the intoning of sutras are the original

bridge for Buddhist disciples to communicate with all Buddhas and bodhisattvas. Prayer is also one of the methods for Buddhists to express how their minds are touched. Praying is the hope for a belief; we depend on vows to have hope for the world, to advance in life, and to achieve complete character. The Ten Great Vows of Samantabhadra, the Twelve Great Vows of Avalokitesvara, and the vows of other bodhisattvas: don't all bodhisattvas rely on vows to attain enlightenment?

Ordinarily, when people pray they only pray for themselves. Before I was twenty years old, I did the same and always prayed to Buddha for blessings, for him to allow me to be intelligent, to progress, to overcome obstacles, and to study Buddhism and smoothly pursue the way.

After I turned twenty and graduated from the Buddhist College, I suddenly felt that what I had been praying to all Buddhas and bodhisattvas for every day was only myself. Was I too selfish? From that moment on, I changed and have since been praying for the health and safety and advances in merits and wisdom of my parents, teachers, relatives, friends, and even some Buddhist devotees.

One day, after turning forty, I paused and reflected upon the past. I discovered that my praying was still a type of selfish, covetous desire, since whatever I had been praying for was "mine": "my" teachers, "my" parents, and "my" friends. My prayers were incomplete, according to the Dharma. Therefore, from the age of forty to the age of fifty my praying experienced another breakthrough. I began to pray for world peace, for the wealth and strength of our nation, and for the safety and happiness of our society, and for the liberation of all beings. During that time, I felt that I myself was practicing what was said in the *Avatamsaka Sutra*: I pray for all beings to be free from suffering, and not merely for my own safety and happiness.

When I turned fifty, a thought suddenly occurred to me: if I needed to pray every day for society and the world to all Buddhas and bodhisattvas, what had I actually done for the world and society? Since then, I have prayed to all Buddhas and bodhisattvas to let me shoulder karmic hindrances and sufferings for all beings of the world, to let me bear the hardships and fickleness of the way of the world, to let me put the great compassion of the Buddha into practice, and to let me learn from the proclamation, instruction, blessing, and joy of the Honorable Tathagata.

Taking initiative and vow is not just a slogan but a kind of cultivation and practice. At first, I vowed to compose a book of prayers; now, with the help of my disciples Man Guo, Man Yi, Man Ji, Jue Liao, and Miao Guang, I can finally accomplish my vow and have this book of prayers published and circulated. So far Nan Tien Temple in Australia has already taken the lead and uses these prayers for morning and evening chanting. Fo Guang Yuan in Singapore has recorded the prayers on CD and now has the CD in circulation. Other places in the world have also collected and published the prayers. In order to unify the collection, I have asked Fo Guang Shan Religious Affairs Committee to assign Venerable Yong Jun of Xiang Hai Publishing and Buddha's Light Publishing to publish a complete edition. This will make the prayers available for all people who are responsive to the Buddha. I hope that everyone will recite one prayer at some time each day, especially in the morning and evening. By doing so, we each will raise our faith to a higher level, advance our compassionate virtues, be able to communicate with all Buddhas and bodhisattvas, and comprehend the needs of the masses of society. I certainly hope that this book of Buddha's Light prayers will become a textbook for cultivating at home. Now that this publication is about to be circulated, I hereby record its conditional causation as above.

Hsing Yun
Fo Guang Shan, Kaohsiung, Taiwan
June 2000

自序

　　六十年前,就是一九三九年的春天,我在棲霞山剃度,那年是十二歲。我經常在更深夜靜的時候,獨自跪在佛堂裏,向佛陀及觀世音菩薩祈求聰明智慧、祈求加持護助,感覺「祈願」的修行,增加了自己的力量,增長了自己的信心。所以,出家六十多年來,一個甲子的歲月,「祈願」一直是自己每天必有的修行。

　　「祈願」又稱「祈禱」,「祈禱」本來就是各個宗教都有的儀式。我從小在叢林古寺裏,初一十五也有正式的「祈禱」。只是當時的「祈禱文」,文長意深,實非初學者所能領會。因此,自己只有依照老師的指導,在早晚祈願:「悉發菩提心,蓮花遍地生,弟子心朦朧,禮拜觀世音,求聰明,拜智慧⋯⋯。」從此在我心中就許下了一個心願,我願為全佛教、全社會撰寫一套普為大眾所通用的「祈願文」。

　　多年來,我曾經試著在盛大的法會中,以及在喜喪婚慶的典禮時,甚至在「家庭普照」的時候,經常都為當事者祈願。因為感於過去大陸對佛菩薩宣讀的「文疏」,以及台灣的「表章」,都是要有腔調來朗誦,非一般人所能為。因此,我採用口語化的「祈願」,一直都覺得效果很好。後來世界各地,佛光弟子們紛紛抄錄,用來做為各種集會的祈願,一般人都說「感人至深」。

　　梵唄經聲,本來就是佛弟子與諸佛菩薩溝通的橋樑;「祈願」也是佛子們表達心中諸多感動的方法。「祈願」就是對信仰的希望,生活中要靠發願,人間才有希望,人生才能增上,人格才能圓滿完成。普賢菩薩的十大願、觀世音菩薩十二大願⋯⋯，菩薩們不都是靠願力才能完成佛道的嗎？

一般人祈願，莫不為自己而求。我在二十歲以前，也跟一般人一樣，總是祈求佛陀加持我，讓我聰明，讓我進步；讓我能衝破一切難關，讓我能順利學佛求道。

到二十歲以後，我從佛學院結業出來，忽然覺得每天都是為著自己向諸佛菩薩求這求那，豈不太自私了嗎？自此以後，我就改為替父母師長、親朋好友，乃至為有緣信徒而祈求，願他們身體平安，福慧增長。

慢慢地，到了四十歲以後，有一天，我反觀自照，發現這仍然是一種自私的貪求。因為所求都是「我的」師長、「我的」父母、「我的」朋友，不盡如法。於是從四十歲到五十歲，我的祈願又有了一番突破，我就為世界和平、國家富強、社會安樂、眾生得度而求。這個時候，自覺自己是在實踐《華嚴經》所說的「但願眾生得離苦，不為自己求安樂」。

當五十歲過去的時候，我又忽然心有所感：每天都要求佛菩薩為世界、為社會，那我自己是做什麼的呢？所以，五十歲以後，我開始祈求諸佛菩薩，讓我來代替天下眾生負擔業障苦難，讓我承受世間人情的辛酸冷暖，讓我來實踐佛陀的大慈大悲，讓我來學習如來世尊的示教利喜。

發心立願不是口號，是一種修行、實踐。當初發願撰寫的「祈願文」，經弟子滿果、滿義、滿濟、

覺了、妙廣等,如今終於「完成所願」,即將出版流通。目前澳洲南天寺已經率先用來做為早晚課誦,新加坡的佛光緣則製作成ＣＤ流通;其他世界各地也都紛紛蒐集印行。為了統一版本。今請佛光山宗務委員會責成香海文化永均法師,以及佛光出版社印行,方便有緣人運用。希望大家每天不拘什麼時候,尤其能在早晚各誦一篇,籍以自我昇華信心、增進慈悲道德,能和諸佛菩薩交流,體會社會大眾的需要。當然,我很希望這本《佛光祈願文》,能成為居家修行的課本。今因流通在即,故錄其緣起如上。

星雲 於佛光山法堂
　　　西元二千年六月(佛光三十四年)

Introduction

Among the many offerings that Buddhists make to the Buddha are incense, flowers, candles, and fruit. We make these offerings out of respect to the Buddha, not because the Buddha demands such offerings or because we expect to be rewarded by the Buddha for our offerings. We also offer ourselves when we bow and prostrate before the Buddha. To this list of offerings we may also add our words in the form of prayers to the Great Compassionate Buddha.

Venerable Master Hsing Yun has written this beautiful and comprehensive collection of Buddhist prayers to help Buddhists of all schools to focus their thoughts and to offer to the Buddha beautiful words of praise, gratitude, and thanksgiving. It is our hope that readers of these prayers will meditate upon the words and how they apply to their lives; will see their situations through the eyes of wisdom; and will act to bring about the changes that they desire in their lives.

On the path towards enlightenment we will receive help from many sources, and prayer or praise offerings will play a major role for many practitioners. It is hoped these special prayers by Venerable Master Hsing Yun will take the reader far along the path towards enlightenment.

Louvenia Ortega
February, 2003

Acknowledgments

We received a lot of help from many people and we want to thank them for their efforts in making the publication of this book possible. We especially appreciate Venerable Tzu Jung, the Chief Executive of Fo Guang Shan International Translation Center (F.G.S.I.T.C.), Venerable Hui Chuan, the Abbot of Hsi Lai Temple, and Venerable Yi Chao, the Director of F.G.S.I.T.C., for their support and leadership; Shujan Cheng and Tom Manzo for their translation; James Baquet, Pey-Rong Lee, and Brenda Bolinger for their editing; Venerable Yi Chao, Venerable Miao Han, Dr. Richard Kimball, Louvenia Ortega, Agnes Ho, and Virginia Wong for their proofreading; Carol Peng, Mei-Chi Shih, and Ching Tay for book and cover design; and Mu-tzen Hsu and Echo Tsai for preparing the manuscript for publication. Our appreciation also goes to everyone who has supported this project from its conception to its completion.

Pearls of Wisdom
佛光祈願文 (2)

Prayers for Engaged Living II

Professions and Society
社會・職業

Buddhism and Dharma Service
佛教・法會

A Prayer for Our Armed Forces

Oh great, compassionate Buddha!
Battle drums roll, cannons rumble,
Wars continue here,
And battles are imminent there;
Some may resort to force as a result of different ideals;
Some struggle and fight with others out of a conflict of interests;
Some may wait for the chance to invade others merely in order to oppress the weak;
Some may occupy others in order to expand their territory;
Some may launch wars in order to wipe away national shame and avenge their nation;
Some may mobilize troops to make a show of force to parade their superiority and competitiveness;
Some may dispatch armies to subdue others in order to uphold justice;
Some may console the people by punishing the wicked and driving out the enemy.

Oh great, compassionate Buddha!
Under the rumbling of cannon and gunfire,
In some places there are people who
Bleed so much on the battlefield
That their blood flows like a river;
In some places the earth is scorched and ravaged by war;

為三軍將士祈願文

慈悲偉大的佛陀！
戰鼓咚咚，炮聲隆隆，
不是這邊烽火連天，
就是那邊戰雲彌漫。
　有的是因為理念不同而兵戎相見，
　有的是因為利益衝突而你爭我奪，
　有的是因為恃強欺弱而伺機侵略，
　有的是因為拓展疆土而侵佔他國，
　有的是因為雪恥復仇而發動戰爭，
　有的是因為逞強好勝而舉兵示威，
　有的是因為伸張正義而興師征討，
　有的是因為驅逐惡寇而弔民伐罪。

慈悲偉大的佛陀！
在炮火槍聲之下，
有的地方血流成河，
有的地方一片焦土。
　多少生靈塗炭，

Many people suffer from extreme privation;
Throngs of homeless and famished people roam the countryside;
Many homes are destroyed;
Many families are broken up.

Oh great, compassionate Buddha!
In the human world, nothing is more precious than life;
Yet war causes some fires of life to be extinguished,
And so many lights of life to be dimmed.

Oh great Buddha!
To defend the nation and protect the people:
Our air force risks the surprise attack of stray bullets;
Our navy battles against surging billows and enemy warships;
Our army fights bloody conflicts on the battlefield;
Our armored troops display their brave, dashing appearance;
And our logistics units provide support behind the lines.
They stand by their posts day and night to maintain battle readiness;
They sacrifice their precious lives in exchange for the people's survival;
They risk their lives, brave untold dangers,

多少哀鴻遍野，
多少人家園被毀，
多少人妻離子散。

慈悲偉大的佛陀！
人間最可貴者無如生命，
但是，戰爭啊！
　讓多少生命之火熄滅了！
　讓多少生命之光黯然了！

偉大的佛陀！
為了保國衛民，
我們的空軍冒著飛彈襲擊的危險，
我們的海軍與惡浪敵艦搏鬥，
我們的陸軍在沙場浴血奮戰，
還有那裝甲戰車勇武的英姿，
還有那聯勤部隊後方的供輸。
他們不分晝夜，枕戈待旦，
　以他們可貴的性命，換取人民大眾的生存；
他們不計危險，出生入死，

And defend the nation's territory with their precious blood.

Oh great, compassionate Buddha!
With your great blessing and support,
May they become invincible warriors, for the preservation of peace;
May they become great heroes, for the promotion of justice.

Oh great, compassionate Buddha!
May our armed forces:
Be able to understand
Both themselves and their opponents, and avoid danger;
Be well-versed
In the art of war and uphold justice;
Be able to exercise compassion and wisdom,
And achieve victory through martial virtues;
Be able to possess courage and kindness,
And win the war without fighting a battle.
May they defend our nation
With the spirit of fearlessness;
May they guard the people
With the courage of great compassion.

Oh great, compassionate Buddha!
Please bless and protect our armed forces;

慈悲偉大的佛陀！
祈求您的大力加持，
　　讓他們成為維護和平的金剛戰士，
　　讓他們成為伸張正義的英雄好漢。

慈悲偉大的佛陀！
願我們的戰士們，
　　都能了解敵我，免於危險；
　　都能善於用兵，主持正義；
　　都能悲智雙運，武德獲勝；
　　都能仁勇兼具，不戰而勝；
　　都能以大無畏的精神，作國家之干城；
　　都能以大慈悲的勇氣，作人民之依怙。

慈悲偉大的佛陀！
請您庇佑我們的戰兒們，

May they be spared from the sacrifice of dying for their country;
May they be free from the misery of illness;
May they be free from the troubles of natural disasters;
May they be free from the infection of serious disease;
May they bring peace and security to the nation;
May they safely return to their families.

Oh great, compassionate Buddha,
Please accept our sincerest prayer!
Oh great, compassionate Buddha,
Please accept our sincerest prayer!

免於殉難的危險，
免於病痛的苦惱，
免於天災的侵擾，
免於疫癘的傳染。
讓他們能夠安邦定國，
讓他們能夠平安歸來。

慈悲偉大的佛陀！
請求您接受我們的祈願！
慈悲偉大的佛陀！
請求您接受我們的祈願！

A Prayer for Explorers

*O*h great, compassionate Buddha!
Please listen to our prayer:
In this world,
There are many people of great wisdom, kindness, and courage;
For the benefit of all humankind:
Some search the deep seas for treasure;
Some prospect in the desert for energy resources;
Some unearth ancient remains in the wilderness;
Some search the high mountains for potential discoveries.
For the welfare of the masses of society,
They risk their lives, only to search for more resources.

However, Buddha!
Among those great explorers:
Some have lost their lives exploring the deep seas;
Some have died in the vast deserts;
Some have been killed by wild beasts;
Some have fallen victim to hazardous mountains and cliffs.

Oh great, compassionate Buddha,
We pray that explorers,
In their difficult journeys of exploration,

為探險者祈願文

慈悲偉大的佛陀！
請您垂聽我的祈求：
在這世間上，
　　有很多大智大仁大勇的人，
他們為了全球人類的利益，
　　有的在深海找尋寶藏，有的在沙漠探勘油礦，
　　有的在曠野挖掘古蹟，有的在高山找尋機緣。
他們為了社會大眾的福祉，冒著性命的危險，
只想為大家找尋更多的資源。

但是，佛陀啊！
那許多偉大的探險者，
　　有的命喪於深海之中，有的暴屍於漠漠黃沙，
　　有的葬身於虎狼之腹，有的罹難於高山深谷。

慈悲偉大的佛陀！
請您讓他們在艱難的探險旅途中，

*May be able to attain great achievement
And return home safely.*

*Oh Buddha!
Please behold those who explore the deep seas:
Sometimes they may be tossed around in the crashing waves;
Sometimes they may struggle in a perilous whirlpool;
They may be surrounded by terrifying sharks;
They may be attacked by vicious sea serpents.
Please behold those who explore the wilderness:
Sometimes they may be entangled by creeping vines and
     thorns;
Sometimes they may be tripped by rocks and branches;
They may be injured and poisoned by exotic flowers and
     unusual plants;
They may be attacked by ferocious beasts at any moment.
Please behold those who explore the desolate desert:
Sometimes they may be lost in the boundless desert;
Sometimes they may lose their direction in the windy and
     swirling desert;
They may be endangered by scorching sun and severe cold;
They may be submerged by windstorms or quicksand.
Please behold those who explore the high mountains:
Sometimes they may be trapped by overhanging precipices
     and steep cliffs;*

能夠獲得偉大的成就，能夠平平安安地回來。

您看深海的探險者，
有時在滔天巨浪中翻騰，
有時在險惡漩渦裡掙扎，
　鯊魚可能張著大口，圍繞身旁；
　海蛇可能吐著紅信，伸向腳下。
您看曠野的探險者，
　有時被蔓藤荊棘糾纏，
　有時被石塊樹枝絆倒。
奇花異草可能讓他們中毒受傷，
凶禽猛獸可能讓他們危在旦夕。
您看荒漠的探險者，
　有時在茫茫黃沙中不知所止，
　有時在飛灰煙瘴中迷失方向，
烈日嚴寒可能奪走他們的性命，
風暴流沙可能淹沒他們的身體。
您看高山的探險者，
　有時在懸崖峭壁中進退兩難，

Sometimes they may be stranded on lofty and precipitous
    peaks;
A strong wind may force them to the bottom of a valley;
A mere accident may cost them their lives.

Oh great, compassionate Buddha!
We pray to you:
May these explorers be able to return home safely;
May these explorers be able to reunite with their families.

Oh great, compassionate Buddha!
In the presence of these great explorers,
We indeed feel humble.
As insignificant as ants in a cave,
We are only busy with our own survival;
As short-sighted as a frog in a well,
We exist only for our own lives.

Oh great, compassionate Buddha!
Kneeling in front of you, we pray:
May we never flinch when experiencing peril;
May we never be disheartened when encountering hardship.
At any moment,

有時在崇山峻嶺間上下無路。
一場颶風可能將他們吹落谷底，
一次意外可能讓他們粉身碎骨。

慈悲偉大的佛陀！
請求您讓這些探險者，
　都能夠平平安安地回家，
　都能夠和妻兒親人團聚。

慈悲偉大的佛陀！
面對這些偉大的探險家，讓我們感到自己的卑微。
我只如洞穴中的螻蟻，為個己的生存忙碌，
我只如井底之蛙，為個己的生命存在。

慈悲偉大的佛陀！
我要在您的座下祈願：
　願我，歷經險惡永不退縮，
　願我，遭逢苦難永不灰心。
願我在每一個當下，

May we be as courageous
As these explorers in their exploration;
May we be as brave
As these explorers during their experiences.

Oh great, compassionate Buddha,
Please accept our pious prayer!
Oh great, compassionate Buddha,
Please accept our pious prayer!

　　和探險家一樣勇於探索；
願我在每一個時刻，
　　和探險家一樣勇於歷練；

慈悲偉大的佛陀！
請求您接受我衷心的祈願！
慈悲偉大的佛陀！
請求您接受我衷心的祈願！

A Prayer for Sanitation Workers

Oh great, compassionate Buddha!
Among all the occupations in the world,
We are deeply thankful for our sanitation workers.
They arise daily earlier than the sun itself,
They are more precise than the clock itself;
Their job is to battle with dirt and refuse,
Their task is to bring cleanliness to the people.

Oh great, compassionate Buddha!
At every dawn,
We hear their brooms cleaning the streets;
At every dusk,
We see their bodies covered with dirt and sweat.
Regardless of the darkness, the cold, the filth, and the foul
    odors,
They tirelessly collect discarded refuse at each place,
They sweep and clear filth from each street.
They risk infection from diseases,
They endure a strenuous workload,
Only so that people
Can enjoy fresh air,
And can see clean streets in the morning.

為清道夫祈願文

慈悲偉大的佛陀！
在人生各行各業當中，
我們最感謝的就是清道夫。
　他們每天比太陽還要早起，
　他們每天比時鐘還要準確，
　他們的工作就是和髒亂奮鬥，
　他們的任務就是將清潔給人。

慈悲偉大的佛陀！
每天清晨，就可以聽到他們掃把沙沙的聲音，
每到黃昏，又看見他們全身的灰塵和汗水，
他們不畏黑夜，不懼寒冷；
他們不嫌髒亂，不怕惡臭。
一站一站地收拾人們不要的垃圾，
一處一處地掃淨街道巷弄的污穢。
他們不懼疾病的傳染，他們不畏工作的繁重，
只為每天一早，當人們推開家門，
　就能嗅到清潔的空氣，就能看到乾淨的道路。

Oh great, compassionate Buddha!
When sanitation workers are engaged in their work,
Speeding cars may pass them dangerously close;
When sanitation workers are removing refuse,
Drunken revelers may attack them.
They often suffer cuts from broken glass,
And punctures from fragments of metal or nails,
And yet they remain undaunted
In turning useless refuse
Into useful resources and fertilizer.

Oh great, compassionate Buddha!
We pray for your support and blessing:
As sanitation workers clean the streets,
May they sweep away the dust of their vexations;
As they tend the trees lining the streets,
May they cultivate the bodhi in their minds;
As they clear away the refuse,
May they eliminate the karma accumulated from their past
          lives;
As they clean ditches and drains,
May they wash away their karmic hindrances.

慈悲偉大的佛陀！
在清道夫工作的時候，
　　汽車從他們身旁急駛而過；
在清道夫清除垃圾的時候，
　　還會遭受醉漢的侵擾；
他們經常為玻璃碎片所傷，
他們經常受鐵絲洋釘所刺，
但是他們仍把人們丟棄的垃圾，
　　重新變換成能源！重新再成為肥料！

慈悲偉大的佛陀！
祈求您的加被，
讓他們在打掃街道的時候，
　　能掃去自己煩惱的塵埃；
讓他們在扶起路樹的時候，
　　能栽植自己心中的菩提；
讓他們在處理垃圾的時候，
　　能消除自己累劫的災殃；
讓他們在清理水溝的時候，
　　能滌除自己往昔的業障。

May they gain respect in society;
May they gain appreciation at home.

Oh Buddha, we pray to you:
May all those in politics
See the sanitation workers' spirit of service;
May all those in education
See the sanitation workers' ability to remove filth;
May all those in finance
See the sanitation workers' virtue of exploring and
    conserving resources;
May all those in health research
See the sanitation workers' role in protecting our minds and
    bodies.

Oh great, compassionate Buddha!
Please protect all sanitation workers:
May their bodies be healthy, safe, and at ease;
May their lives be happy and their wishes fulfilled;

請讓他們在社會上，
　　能受到大家的尊敬；
請讓他們在居家時，
　　能受到家人的讚賞。

祈求您讓所有的政治學家，
　　學習清道夫為民服務的精神；
祈求您讓所有的教育學家，
　　學習清道夫除去污穢的能力；
祈求您讓所有的經濟學家，
　　學習清道夫開源節流的美德；
祈求您讓所有的病理學家，
　　學習清道夫加強身心的保健。

慈悲偉大的佛陀！
祈求您保護所有的清道夫
　　讓他們的身體健康，平安自在；
　　讓他們的生活美滿，所求如意。

May their world be joyous and harmonious;
May their future be secure and wonderful.

Oh great, compassionate Buddha,
Please accept our sincerest prayer!
Oh great, compassionate Buddha,
Please accept our sincerest prayer!

祈求您保護所有的清道夫
　讓他們的世界快樂而祥和，
　讓他們的未來平安而美好！

慈悲偉大的佛陀！
請您接受我至誠的祈求，
慈悲偉大的佛陀！
請您接受我至誠的祈求。

A Prayer for Farmers, Fishery Workers, and Laborers

Oh great, compassionate Buddha!
We would like to express our heartfelt thanks
To farmers, fishery workers, and laborers;
We would like to offer
Our prayers and blessings for them.
Because of them,
Our people do indeed live in affluence;
Our country does indeed exist in security;
Our society's economy does indeed progress and prosper;
Our industries do indeed expand steadily.

Oh great, compassionate Buddha!
Have you witnessed the hardship of farmers?
The attack of a single storm
Can cause them disastrous loss,
The ravages of one insect pest
Can make their efforts fruitless.
A farmer must go through many seasons of trial
To enjoy a bountiful harvest.

Oh great, compassionate Buddha!
Have you ever listened to the hearts of fishery workers?

為農漁勞工祈願文

慈悲偉大的佛陀！
我要向農漁勞工表示由衷的感謝，
我要向農漁勞工提出祈願與祝福，
因為有了他們，
人類的生活才得以豐衣足食，
國家的存在才得以安和樂利，
社會的經濟才得以繁榮進步，
實業的發展才得以穩定成長。

慈悲偉大的佛陀！
您可曾看到農民的辛酸？
一次的風雨來襲，可能讓他們損失慘重；
一次的害蟲肆虐，可能讓他們心血白費。
作為一個農民，他必須經過多少次寒暑的考驗，
　　才能享受豐碩的收成！

慈悲偉大的佛陀！
　　您可曾聽過漁民的心聲？

Although they are engaged in ending the lives of beings,
They do indeed endure a hard life.
Those who are engaged in marine fisheries
May be swept by huge, pounding waves, or
May be devoured by sharks.
For those who breed fish for market,
The contamination of one stretch of water
May result in no return on their hard-earned investment;
The infectious spread of but one epidemic
May exhaust their wealth.

Oh Buddha! Buddha!
We pray to you to understand them:
Because they possess the karma resulting from killing,
But do not kill for killing's sake.
We pray to you to forgive
The demerits made necessary by survival.

Oh great, compassionate Buddha!
Have you realized the hardship of laborers?
The occurrence of one accident
May cause the entire family to lose support;
The occurrence of one work-related injury
May immobilize them and make them unable to earn a living.

他們做的是殺害的行為，
　　但他們過的是辛苦的生活。
從事海洋漁業的人，
　　惡浪可能把他們捲走，鯊魚可能將他們吞噬。
從事養殖漁業的人，
一次廢水污染，可能讓他們血本無歸；
一次瘟疫傳染，可能讓他們傾家蕩產。

佛陀啊！佛陀！
祈求您包容他們雖有殺業，但沒有殺心；
祈求您寬恕他們求生的功過。

慈悲偉大的佛陀！
　　您可曾了解勞工的艱難？
一次的意外發生，
　　可能讓他全家生活沒有著落；
一次的職業病變，
　　可能讓他倒臥在床無法工作。

Laborers must endure the tempering of numerous adversities
So they can succeed in their occupations.

Oh great, compassionate Buddha!
We would like to pray for our farmers, fishery workers, and laborers:
May our nation give them more care;
May our government show them more favor;
May our society show them more concern;
May our people give them more help.

Oh great, compassionate Buddha!
We pray that all farmers, fishery workers, and laborers of the world be able to:
Have the heart of willingness to benefit the masses;
Bring into full play the virtue of helping and cooperating with each other;
Find the courage to overcome all adversities;
Have the ambition to improve and create.
We also pray that you bless all people in the world:
May they see the willingness of farmers, fishery workers, and laborers
To do their jobs honestly and with dedication,

作為一個勞工，
他必須經過多少次困境的淬煉，
　才能擁有成功的事業！

慈悲偉大的佛陀！
我要為農漁勞工祈願，
　希望國家能給他們多一點照顧，
　希望政府能給他們多一點優惠，
　希望社會能給他們多一點關懷，
　希望大眾能給他們多一點協助。

慈悲偉大的佛陀！
我祈願天下所有的農漁勞工，
　都能擁有福利大眾的願心，
　都能發揮互助合作的美德，
　都能鼓舞突破困難的勇氣，
　都能具有改良創新的抱負。
更祈求您，
　加被天下所有的人，
學習農漁勞工腳踏實地的精神，

And try to create happiness and benefit for humankind;
May they see the willingness of farmers, fishery workers, and laborers
To be simple, sincere, and honest,
And create a wonderful future for the world.

Oh great, compassionate Buddha,
Please accept our pious prayer!
Oh great, compassionate Buddha,
Please accept our pious prayer!

為人類謀求幸福的利益；
學習農漁勞工純樸敦厚的精神，
　為世界創造美好的未來。

慈悲偉大的佛陀！
請求您接受我至誠的祈願，
慈悲偉大的佛陀！
請求您接受我至誠的祈願。

A Prayer for Health-Care Professionals

Oh great, compassionate Buddha!
How dreadful it is to speak about these things:
Most people in this world suffer
Torment from some illness;
Some suffer the physical illnesses
Of old age, sickness, and death;
Some suffer mentally through the weaknesses
Of greed, anger, and ignorance.

Only you, Buddha, are the world's great doctor;
You are able to help people not only recover physically,
But also to help them heal mentally.
Furthermore, you encourage us to tend to the sick.
You once told us,
"Of the eight fields of merit,
"Tending to the sick is the greatest."
You also encouraged outstanding nursing professionals:
First, not to be deterred by foul smells;
Second, to treat the sick with attentiveness;
Third, to dispense medicine;
Fourth, to be adept at preaching the Dharma.
And indeed, since ancient times,
These are the goals that health-care professionals have
      pursued.

為醫護人員祈願文

慈悲偉大的佛陀！
說來是多麼的恐懼！
這個世間上的人多數都患有病苦，
　有的身體上患了老病死的疾病，
　有的心理上患了貪瞋癡的毛病。

唯有佛陀您是世界上最偉大的醫王，
您不但能助人病體康復，
　而且能助人心病痊癒。
甚至，您還鼓勵我們探視病苦，
告訴我們：
　「八福田中，探病為第一福田。」
您也鼓勵優秀的護理人員：
　一要不嫌穢氣，二要看護細心，
　三要調和湯藥，四要善於說法。
自古以來，
　這些都是醫護人員追求的目標。

Oh great, compassionate Buddha!
Many health-care professionals have followed in your steps
To fill our days with goodwill.
Oh Buddha, those doctors who are kindhearted
And benevolent in deeds are like you;
They make house calls to treat patients
As soon as they hear about the seriously ill;
They rush to help patients
As soon as they know of their injuries.
Those nurses who give themselves completely
To fulfill their duties are like Avalokitesvara Bodhisattva:
Their uplifting and efficient figures
Shuttle back and forth deftly between sickbeds,
Hoping only to bring comfort to patients;
They toil day and night to care for patients,
Wishing only to ensure their rapid recovery.
What their ears hear are the groans of patients;
Yet their hands have to be busy tending patients;
What their eyes see is the anguish of patients,
Yet their mouths still speak comforting and loving words.
Upon seeing the worsening condition of patients,
The mood of the health-care professional is also lowered;
Only upon seeing the full recovery of patients
Do health-care professionals relax their concern.
Health-care professionals work irregular hours;

慈悲偉大的佛陀！
許多醫護人員追隨您的腳步，
　　為人間寫下了溫馨的歷史。
仁心仁術的醫生如同佛陀一樣，
　　一聽到急症病人，馬上出診治療；
　　一知道受傷患者，立刻前往救助。
克盡職責的護士如同觀音菩薩，
他們輕巧的身影穿梭在病床之間，
　　只希望為患者帶來安心；
他們不分晝夜辛苦地守護著病人，
　　只為了讓患者早日康寧。
他們耳裡聽到的是病人的呻吟，
他們手裡必須忙著病人的診斷；
他們眼裡看到的是患者的苦臉，
他們口裡還要說著安慰的愛語。
當醫護人員看到病人痊癒時，心中的掛念才放下來；
當醫護人員看到病人危險時，情緒也隨之寞落低沉。
醫護人員的作息無法定時，
　　甚至冒著感染的危險，
　　甚至犧牲家人的聚會。

They even risk the possibility of infection,
And sacrifice time with their families.
After a full day of making rounds and inspecting wards,
Their leg muscles often ache from fatigue;
After a full day of performing surgical operations,
They are often about to collapse from exhaustion.

We pray to you, Buddha, to support and protect health-care professionals:
May they be able to have strong and healthy bodies;
May they be able to have perfect medical skills;
May their families appreciate their hard work;
May their relatives and friends support their ideals.

Oh great, compassionate Buddha!
We would like to pray for health-care professionals:
May they persevere,
And carry out everything without obstacles;
May they always smile,
And have their wishes fulfilled;
May they be compassionate and wise,
And help patients to have quick recoveries;
May they be mindful of their own health,
And stay well both physically and mentally.

他們一天巡視病房下來，
　　往往兩腳酸麻；
他們一天執行手術下來，
　　常常疲憊不堪。

祈求佛陀加被醫護人員，
　　讓他們能擁有強健的身體，
　　讓他們能擁有精湛的醫術，
　　讓他們的家人能體諒他們的辛苦，
　　讓他們的親友能支持他們的理想。

慈悲偉大的佛陀！
我要為醫護人員祈願——
　　希望他們耐力堅強，事事順遂；
　　希望他們笑口常開，所求如願；
　　希望他們慈悲靈巧，藥到病除；
　　希望他們注意保健，身心愉快。

Oh great, compassionate Buddha!
Suffering patients trust their lives and health
To the hands of health-care professionals;
The extraordinary health-care professionals
Devote their time and energy to patients;
May all health-care professionals and their families
Enjoy extended happiness and longevity,
And be peaceful, safe, and fortunate.

Oh great, compassionate Buddha,
Please accept our pious prayer!
Oh great, compassionate Buddha,
Please accept our pious prayer!

慈悲偉大的佛陀！
痛苦的病人將生命、健康
　　交到醫護人員手裡，
偉大的醫護人員將時間、青春奉獻給了病人。
願醫護人員以及他們的家人，
　　都能福壽綿延，都能平安吉祥。

慈悲偉大的佛陀！
請求您接受我至誠的祈願！
慈悲偉大的佛陀！
請求您接受我至誠的祈願！

A Prayer for Police Officers

Oh great, compassionate Buddha!
With the utmost sincerity,
We would like to pray
For the protectors of the people: the police officers.
They may not be tall and strong,
Yet they must have steadfast courage;
They may not be in positions of power,
Yet they have to be responsible for bringing safety to the people;
They may not receive the glory of heroes,
Yet they have to possess the spirit of bravery;
They may not have a generous income,
Yet they have to ensure the safety and peace of society.

Oh great, compassionate Buddha!
It is the police officers who return to parents
The youths who have wandered the streets;
It is the police officers who pursue villains
Who have done crimes in violation of the law;
It is the police officers who have the task
Of protecting innocent, victimized people;
It is the police officers who bear the responsibility
Of restoring harmony in disputes between neighbors.

為警察祈願文

慈悲偉大的佛陀！
我要為人民的保姆——警察，
　　至誠懇切向您祈願。
因為，
他們沒有魁梧的身軀，卻需要具備堅毅的勇氣；
他們沒有強勢的地位，卻需要負起安民的責任；
他們沒有英雄的標章，卻需要富有冒險的精神；
他們沒有優厚的收入，卻需要帶給社會的安全。

慈悲偉大的佛陀！
流浪街頭的少年，是警察將他們交給父母；
為非作歹的壞人，是警察將他們繩之以法；
無辜受害的百姓，是警察扮演保護的角色；
鄉里居民的糾紛，是警察擔當協調的責任。

Oh great, compassionate Buddha!
May they embody your prajna wisdom
To solve thorny and difficult cases;
May they embody your great power
To subdue stubborn and unruly criminals;
May they embody your compassion and fellow-feeling
To guide all beings that take the wrong path;
May they embody your steadfast determination
To maintain the courage and wisdom to advance.

Oh great, compassionate Buddha!
In their regular duties,
They work both day and night,
And brave the harshness of severe weather;
They firmly stand their posts, and patrol the streets.
No matter whether at dawn, at dusk, or late at night,
They risk their lives and remain undaunted by hard work;
They defy all difficulties and dangers to carry out their duties.
Even in dangerous places,
They never allow criminals to remain beyond the law's reach;
Even overseas,
They can arrest and extradite criminals.

Oh great, compassionate Buddha!
Police officers are only human;
They need adequate rest;

慈悲偉大的佛陀！
願他們能擁有您的般若智慧，破解棘手難辦的案件；
願他們能擁有您的大雄大力，降伏頑強無知的罪犯；
願他們能擁有您的同體慈悲，導引誤入歧途的眾生；
願他們能擁有您的堅忍毅力，保有勇於前進的膽識。

慈悲偉大的佛陀！
他們在平常服勤的時候，
　　不分晝夜，不分寒暑，堅守崗位，巡視街頭；
他們在晨昏深夜的時候，
　　不計身命，不計勞苦；赴湯蹈火，執行任務。
他們在任何險地，
　　都不讓罪犯逍遙法外；
他們在國際海外，
　　都能將罪犯逮捕歸來。

慈悲偉大的佛陀！
警察也是血肉凡軀，
　　他們需要適當的休息，

They need proper entertainment;
They need family support;
They need the hope of safety.

Oh Buddha, with your great power we pray for your blessings:
May police officers have
Both wisdom and bravery to serve the people;
May they have strong resolve
To defend home and country.

Furthermore, we pray to you to bless and protect our society:
May we all serve as police officers
To keep watch together in mutual defense, and collaborate
    closely with each other;
May we all uphold justice and prevent crimes,
And bring peace and safety to all families;
May we all be self-disciplined and law-abiding
To bring happiness to our lives, and prosperity and peace to
    our nation;
May we all firmly stand by our posts
To contribute to the community and to benefit our society.

他們需要正當的娛樂；
他們需要家庭的支持，
他們需要安全的保障。

我們祈求您的大力加被，
讓他們能夠智勇雙全，為民服務；
讓他們能夠心力堅忍，保家衛國。

更祈求您庇佑我們的社會，
讓人人都能擔當警察，守望相助，合作無間；
讓人人都能伸張正義，打擊罪犯，家家平安；
讓人人都能自律守法，生活幸福，國家康莊；
讓人人都能堅守崗位，奉獻人群，造福社會。

Oh great, compassionate Buddha,
Please accept our sincerest prayer!
Oh great, compassionate Buddha,
Please accept our sincerest prayer!

慈悲偉大的佛陀！
請求您接受我至誠的祈願，
慈悲偉大的佛陀！
請求您接受我至誠的祈願。

A Prayer for Our Volunteers

Oh great, compassionate Buddha!
We would sincerely like to report to you:
In our society, there is a group of respectable volunteers
Who add honor and vitality to this indifferent age,
Who pour passion and justice into this disillusioned society.

While others feverishly pursue power,
They serve in humble silence;
While others negotiate for fame and position,
They unceasingly offer kindness.

Though they do not aim for rewards,
They earn merit and joy;
Though they do not wish for fame and position,
They become the friends that others welcome the most.

Oh great, compassionate Buddha!
After work,
While others are relaxing at home,

為義工祈願文

慈悲偉大的佛陀！
我要虔誠地向您稟告：
社會裡有一群可敬的義工朋友，
　為機械冷漠的時代增添了光熱，
　為人情紙薄的潮流注入了情義。

當別人蜂湧追求權力時，
　他們默默為人服務；
當別人爭執計較名位時，
　他們不斷付出愛心。

他們的目的雖然不是為了報酬，
　卻為自己賺到了功德與歡喜；
他們的願望雖然不是為了名位，
　卻讓自己成為最受歡迎的朋友。

慈悲偉大的佛陀！
當公餘之暇，

Our admirable volunteers, like never-resting bodhisattvas,
Contribute their time to charitable associations,
Serve others in temples
And places that teach the Dharma,
Serve as crossing guards,
And support aid organizations to provide disaster relief.

In leisure,
While others are sightseeing and entertaining themselves,
Our lovable volunteers, like ever-diligent bodhisattvas,
Engage in environmental protection in their communities,
Assist mentally-challenged people,
Care for and help the elderly,
And provide free diagnoses and medical treatment.

Oh great, compassionate Buddha!
Our volunteers devote their time and effort to people,
Only wishing that everybody
May live and work in peace and contentment.

I would like to pray for our volunteers,
That their dedication to enlightenment may never change,
And that their commitment to others may never waver.

人們在家裡享受休閒時，
可佩的義工們如同不休息菩薩，
　　有的到福利社團奉獻己力，
　　有的到寺院道場服務大眾，
　　有的在馬路上指揮交通，
　　有的隨各單位四處救災。

當休閒期間，遊人到各地娛樂觀光時，
可愛的義工們如同常精進菩薩，
　　有的從事社區環保，有的協助智障人士，
　　有的幫忙照顧老人，有的義務施診醫療。

佛陀！偉大的佛陀！
義工們為人群奉獻時間與心力，
他們不為什麼，
　　只希望大家能夠安居樂業。

我要為義工們祈願，
希望他們道心不變，信念不退，
　　給貪婪的社會留下榜樣，

May they set an example for this materialistic society;
May they create an ideal for selfish people.

Our volunteers toil everywhere,
Apparently exhausting themselves;
But actually, they are the most joyous people.
Our volunteers work for the sake of others,
Apparently benefiting only others;
But actually, they gain the greatest reward.

Oh Buddha! In fact
You are the founder of volunteerism,
You are the model for volunteers.
For the benefit and liberation of sentient beings
You progressed diligently over many kalpas,
And practiced the most austere cultivation;
Even right before you entered parinirvana
You still persisted in teaching
In order to help sentient beings attain enlightenment.

Oh great, compassionate Buddha!
Before one attains Buddhahood,
One must first serve all sentient beings.
All bodhisattvas attain bodhi through volunteer work:

給自私的行為留下模範。

義工們到處奔跑，
　好像很辛苦，
　　其實他們是最快樂的人；
義工們為人著想，
　好像在利他，
　　其實他們是最大的收穫者。

佛陀！其實，
您就是義工的祖師，
您就是義工的模範。
您為了利濟有情眾生，
累劫精進，難行能行；
甚至涅槃前，仍拖著病軀度眾。

慈悲偉大的佛陀！
　欲作佛門龍象，先作眾生馬牛。
　菩薩都從義工服務中成就菩提：

Amitabha Buddha volunteered to protect
The Western Pure Land environment;
Medicine Buddha volunteered to promote
The welfare of the Eastern Pure Land,
Avalokitesvara Bodhisattva volunteered to liberate
Those in the vast sea of suffering;
Ksitigarbha Bodhisattva volunteered to relieve
Those suffering in hell.

Oh great, compassionate Buddha!
With your support and blessing, we pray:
That we may acquire the spirit of our volunteers
So that the future increases in reasonableness and
　　　　　righteousness;
That we may promote the virtue of our volunteers
So that the future becomes unified in justice and truth.

Oh great, compassionate Buddha,
Please accept our pious prayer!
Oh great, compassionate Buddha,
Please accept our pious prayer!

阿彌陀佛是極樂淨土的環保義工，
藥師如來是琉璃世界的社福義工，
觀世音菩薩是茫茫苦海中的義工，
地藏王菩薩是熱惱煉獄裡的義工。

慈悲偉大的佛陀！
祈求您的佛光加被，
我們要學習義工的精神，
　　希望未來在有情有義中進步成長，
我們要發揚義工的美德，
　　希望未來在公理正義中合為一家。

慈悲偉大的佛陀！
請求您接受我至誠的祈願，
慈悲偉大的佛陀！
請求您接受我至誠的祈願。

A Prayer for Construction Professionals

Oh great, compassionate Buddha!
With sincere gratitude
We are here to pray to you to bless and protect
Our hard-working construction professionals.
Because:
Residential homes and public facilities,
The development of cities and the construction of the nation,
Places of leisure and halls of culture,
Skyscrapers and factories,
Transportation and industry—
All endeavors related to the people's livelihood
Rely on construction professionals to complete them.

Oh great, compassionate Buddha!
Those wise and brave construction professionals
Are unperturbed by the scorching sun, severe wind, or pouring rain;
They stand fast by their posts and never retreat;
They are like manifestations of bodhisattvas,
Offering themselves for the benefit of the masses.

為工程人員祈願文

慈悲偉大的佛陀！
我在此以感恩的心情向您訴願，
祈求您庇佑辛勞的工程人員們。
因為，
　　從私人住家到公共設施，
　　從城鄉發展到國家建設，
　　從休閒場所到文化殿堂，
　　從大樓、工廠到交通、企業，
所有攸關民生的事業，
　　都是依靠工程人員才能完成。

慈悲偉大的佛陀！
　　那些智勇雙全的工程人員們，
　　不畏烈日當頭，不怕風吹雨打，
　　堅守崗位，從不退卻。
他們就像是菩薩的化身，
　　奉獻自己，利益大眾。

Oh great, compassionate Buddha!
We pray to you to support
All construction professionals:
May they develop the wisdom of prajna;
May they embrace the radiance of faith.

Oh great, compassionate Buddha!
Construction professionals work hard in every possible way:
Some of them enter into deep, dark caves;
Some of them climb steep, high mountains;
Some of them carry heavy gravel and stones on their shoulders;
Some of them operate sophisticated machinery.
They do their work honestly and with dedication;
Each pebble, each stone, each brick, each tile,
Each plan, and each blueprint contribute to
A majestic and imposing building;
It is directly the result of their concerted effort.

Oh great, compassionate Buddha!
Construction professionals are also only human:
Some of them are bedridden due to constant overwork,
And are unable to realize their very promising aspirations;
Some of them lose their lives due to the dangers inherent in
       their occupation,
Resulting in tragedy beyond repair;

慈悲偉大的佛陀！
祈求您加被所有的工程人員，
　　讓他們都能擁有般若的智慧，
　　讓他們懷抱迎向光明的信心。

慈悲偉大的佛陀！
工程人員辛苦備至，
　　有的深入漆黑的岩洞，有的攀爬高聳的山峰，
　　有的肩挑沉重的砂石，有的操控繁複的機械。
他們腳踏實地的工作，
　　那一砂一石，一磚一瓦，
　　那一張計劃，一幅藍圖，
　　所完成的巍峨堂皇的建築，
　　就是他們通力合作的成果。

慈悲偉大的佛陀！
工程人員也是血肉凡軀，他們——
　　有的因積勞成疾，臥病在床，
　　　無法完成遠大的抱負；
　　有的因操作不慎，為公捐軀，
　　　導致無法彌補的遺憾；

Some of them carelessly become involved in corruption cases,
Intending to profit unfairly from others,
Due to inexperience in the affairs of the world;
Some of them meet with the difficult situation of unemployment,
Of being laid off during economic recession,
Due to unfavorable conditions in life.

Oh Buddha! Please bless and protect all construction professionals,
Please grant them wisdom and safety:
May they be free from injuries at work;
May they be free from the temptations of the world;
May they be free from the effects of the economy;
May they be free from the perplexities of unemployment.
Please look:
The Cross-Island Highway in Taiwan,[1]
The damming of the Three Gorges of the Yangtze River,[2]
The Imperial Tsing Ma Bridge[3] in Hong Kong,
The skyscrapers in New York City,
And other great construction projects,
Are all the result of construction professionals
Who toiled unceasingly.

有的因涉世未深，
　　一不小心捲入圖利他人的弊案；
有的因際遇不佳，
　　遭逢經濟衰退裁員失業的困境。

祈求您庇佑所有的工程人員，
賜給他們智慧與平安，
　　讓他們免於工作的傷害，
　　讓他們免於世間的誘惑，
　　讓他們免於經濟的影響，
　　讓他們免於失業的困擾。
您看！
　　台灣的東西橫貫公路[1]，長江三峽[2]的大壩工程，
　　香港的青衣大橋[3]，紐約的摩天大廈，
還有更多偉大的建設，
都是工程人員日以繼夜，拋灑血淚的成果。

Oh great, compassionate Buddha!
Please support all construction professionals with your great power:
May they have the spirit of doing good deeds to benefit humankind,
May they have the virtue of contributing to humankind.

Oh great, compassionate Buddha,
Please accept our sincerest prayer!
Oh great, compassionate Buddha,
Please accept our sincerest prayer!

慈悲偉大的佛陀！
祈求您加被所有的工程人員，
　　讓他們都能擁有造福人群的精神，
　　讓他們都能具備奉獻人群的美德。

慈悲偉大的佛陀！
請求您接受我至誠的祈願，
慈悲偉大的佛陀！
請求您接受我至誠的祈願。

A Prayer for Emergency Rescue and Relief Workers

Oh great, compassionate Buddha!
"In nature there are unexpected storms,
"While in life there is unpredictable fortune and misfortune."
In this world we have suffered
Not only natural disasters, but also man-made calamities;
One catastrophe after another,
We are forever deprived of places of safe refuge.
In each occurrence of natural disaster or man-made calamities,
There have been material losses to society
Beyond measure;
There have been losses in lives, and distressed minds
Beyond repair.

Oh great, compassionate Buddha!
This clearly explains
Why we need kindhearted and righteous people
To relieve the suffering and the distressed,
Why we need kindhearted bodhisattvas
To appear and help with compassion.

Oh Buddha, please look:
In earthquakes, hometowns are destroyed

為救難人員祈願文

慈悲偉大的佛陀！
「天有不測風雲，人有旦夕禍福。」
我們這個世間，
　　不是天災，就是人禍；
　　不是人禍，就是天災；
重重的苦難，不知道安全在何方？
每次天災人禍，
　　社會財物的損失，無以計數；
　　人命心靈的創傷，難以彌補。

慈悲偉大的佛陀！
這說明了
我們需要救苦救難的仁人義士，
我們需要慈悲拔濟的善心菩薩。

你看——
　　地震，家園毀壞，人命無常；

And human life becomes threatened;
During typhoons, torrential rain does rampant damage,
And houses and mountains collapse;
In disastrous fires, firefighting facilities are insufficient
And passages are blocked;
During wars, cannonballs and bullets fly all over
And lives are sacrificed senselessly.
Sometimes we suffer accidents on land, sea, or air;
Sometimes we face the danger of expeditions in the wilderness;
Sometimes we experience the sudden outbreak of riots;
Sometimes we are faced with threats by street thugs;
But when the emergency rescue and relief workers appear,
The rescuers become heroes.

Oh great, compassionate Buddha!
Whenever a disaster occurs,
Some rescue workers search for and rescue casualties;
Some comfort the victims of disaster;
Some bandage and treat the injured;
Some deliver necessities.
They endeavor to the best of their ability to relieve the
    distressed and the suffering;
They arduously travel over passes and through valleys;
They scale mountains and ford streams tirelessly;
They risk their lives without hesitation, and brave untold
    dangers;

颱風，暴雨肆虐，屋倒山崩；
火災，消防不夠，通路阻塞；
戰爭，槍炮子彈，無謂犧牲。
有的人遭到舟車航空的意外，
有的人發生野外登山的危險，
有的人遇到暴動突然的發生，
有的人遇到歹徒劫持的行動，
這時候救難人員的出現，
　他們就是英雄。

慈悲偉大的佛陀！
每當災難來臨，
救難人員們──
　有的忙著搜救傷亡，有的忙著安撫災民，
　有的忙著包紮醫療，有的忙著運送飲食。
他們盡己所能，救苦救難；
　不懼艱辛，攀峰越嶺；
　不怕疲累，跋山涉水；
　不惜身命，出生入死；

They defy all hazards and difficulties in spite of the dangers.

Oh great, compassionate Buddha!
You must know the struggle of these emergency rescue and
 relief workers;
You must understand their hardships.
For during your numerous lifetimes in cultivation,
You once sacrificed your own body
As food to relieve a famine;
You once sacrificed your own body
As medicine in a plague.
Furthermore,
You once risked your life to kill bandits
In order to save five hundred merchants;
You once tirelessly carried water in your mouth
To put out a fire in order to save wildlife in a forest.
Even after you attained Buddhahood,
You did not neglect even small good deeds:
Not only did you go to disaster areas to preach the Dharma and
 console victims,
You also cared for the injured and dispensed medicine.

Oh Buddha! You once told us to
"Serve as guardians to those without protection,
"Serve as rescuers to the helpless."

不計危害，赴湯蹈火。

慈悲偉大的佛陀！
救難人員的辛苦，您一定知道；
救難人員的艱難，您一定了解；
因為佛陀您在因地修行時，
　　曾為解除饑荒，捨身為食；
　　曾為救濟疾疫，施身為藥。
甚至——
您曾為了拯救五百位商人，
　　不顧危險，縛賊殺敵；
您曾為了拯救森林鳥獸，
　　不計疲累，啣水滅火。
即使您成佛之後，仍不辭小善，
　　不但赴往災區，說法慰問；
　　而且照顧病患，餵食湯藥。

佛陀！您曾昭示我們：
　　「無護者，為作護者；無救者，為作救者。」

In this world full of disasters,
Our emergency rescue and relief workers manifest your
  compassionate heart and vows,
Bringing hope to all suffering beings.
They fill this misfortune-ridden world with warmth;
They inspire this impurity-filled world with hope.

We thus pray to you, Buddha, to support them:
May their benevolent minds remain committed;
May their reward for these good deeds be boundless;
May they be blessed with joy and good fortune,
Life after life.

Oh great, compassionate Buddha,
Please accept our sincerest prayer!
Oh great, compassionate Buddha,
Please accept our sincerest prayer!

在這個危難重重的世間裡，
由於救難人員實踐您的慈心悲願，
　布施無畏給苦難的眾生，
　讓多災的人間充滿了溫馨，
　為五濁的惡世帶來了希望。

祈求佛陀您能加被他們，
　善心不退，果報無邊；
　生生世世，吉祥如意。

慈悲偉大的佛陀！
請求您接受我至誠的祈願，
慈悲偉大的佛陀！
請求您接受我至誠的祈願。

A Prayer for Firefighters

Oh great, compassionate Buddha!
People who live in cities
Face either the dangers of city traffic
Or face incidents of fire.
The frequency of disastrous fire is especially frightening:
Over here, some tall building is on fire;
Over there, some restaurant is burning;
The loss of property certainly makes people sad,
But the loss of life and health is even more devastating,
And causes people regret for their entire lives.
When fire breaks out,
It is fortunate when firefighters arrive at the scene in time
To minimize the loss.

Oh great, compassionate Buddha!
These firefighters always take action immediately,
The moment they hear the alarm:
Some of them ride on the fire engine;
Some of them drive the ladder truck.
They do not concentrate on the greatness of their efforts,
But only on how to save people.

為消防人員祈願文

慈悲偉大的佛陀！
居住在都市裡的人們，
　不是怕市虎汽車的危險，
　就是怕火蛇竄起的意外。
尤其，火災迅速，駭人聽聞，
不是這裡的高樓起火，
就是那裡的餐廳焚燒，
失去財物固然令人傷心，
殘廢喪命更是終生遺恨。
當火災發生時，
所幸消防人員及時趕到，
讓損失減到最低的程度。

慈悲偉大的佛陀！
那些消防人員啊！
他們一聽到警報，就立即全隊出動，
有的乘坐消防車，有的駕著雲梯車，
他們不計辛勞，只為救人第一。

Oh great, compassionate Buddha!
These firefighters often enter buildings engulfed in flames
To relieve the distressed and suffering,
Regardless of their own personal safety.
They steady damaged pillars with their own hands
And wade through a sea of fire:
Some of them are busy carrying heavy hoses
To discharge water from down below;
Some of them are busy climbing to the roofs
Of burning buildings to repress the fire from above;
Some of them are busy scaling ladders
To rescue people;
Some of them are busy clearing threatening obstacles
And prying open doors and windows.
They disregard untold dangers and the inexorable advance of
    the burning fire,
Bent only on helping people;
While rescuing victims,
Some of them are burned, with wounds all over their bodies;
While saving property,
Some of them are almost suffocated by thick streams of smoke.
At the scene of hurricanes and tornadoes,
Firefighters always lend a helping hand;
In the disaster area of earthquakes and car accidents,

慈悲偉大的佛陀！
那些消防人員，
在火窟危樓下，
他們奮不顧身，救苦救難。
他們雙手頂著樑柱，
他們腳下就是火海。
有的忙著扛起龍頭，從下面噴射；
有的忙著爬上屋頂，從高空灌灑；
有的忙著攀登雲梯，將人救出；
有的忙著清除障礙，撬開門窗。
他們不顧火燒的危險，
他們不計祝融的無情，
　一心一意只為民眾奉獻；
他們有的為了助人逃生，
　自己卻被烈火燒得遍體鱗傷；
他們有的為了搶救物品，
　自己卻被濃煙嗆得呼吸困難；
在風災、水災的現場，
　消防人員總是伸出援手；
在地震、車禍的災區，

The fire department always offers help.
Upon learning that mountain climbers are in danger
    or that a tourist boat has capsized,
Firefighters always arrive promptly to the rescue;
Even when a wasp or a snake attacks,
Firefighters are always called in to head off the danger.
Firefighters seem to live in the company of danger;
Firefighters and suffering seem to be one.

Oh great, compassionate Buddha!
Please grant firefighters strength,
And that disasters may be prevented entirely;
Please grant firefighters the courage
To avert threats to peace and safety;
Please grant firefighters confidence
To realize that saving lives is a great merit;
Please grant firefighters protection
To change suffering into great fortune.
May firefighters win the applause of the masses;
May firefighters be awarded society's highest honors.

Oh great, compassionate Buddha,
Please accept our sincerest prayer!
Oh great, compassionate Buddha,
Please accept our sincerest prayer!

消防大隊總是出動幫忙；有人在登山時遇難，
有人在遊湖時翻船，消防人員聞聲即來；
一窩虎頭蜂放肆，一條青竹蛇咬人，
　也要找消防人員解危。
消防人員好像和危險結伴，
消防人員彷彿與苦難一體。

慈悲偉大的佛陀！
請您賜給消防人員力量，讓災難消弭於無形；
請您賜給消防人員勇敢，將危險轉為平安；
請您賜給消防人員信心，救人就是大功德；
請您賜給消防人員保佑，苦難轉為大吉祥。
讓消防人員贏得大眾的喝采，
讓消防人員受到社會的勳章。

慈悲偉大的佛陀！
請求您接受我誠摯的祈願！
慈悲偉大的佛陀！
請求您接受我誠摯的祈願！

A Prayer for Performing Artists

Oh great, compassionate Buddha!
In contemporary society,
There is a profession that deserves to be taken more
    seriously—
It is that of the performing artist.

Oh great, compassionate Buddha!
We praise performing artists,
Not in envy of their glamorous outer appearances,
But in honor of their consummate performances.
We praise performing artists,
Not in envy of their actions on the stage,
But in homage to their expressions of honest feelings.

Oh great, compassionate Buddha!
In order to have perfect and moving performances,
Performing artists must endure many trials;
In order create life-like effects,
Performing artists do not hesitate to risk their
    personal safety.
Sometimes they must dash through fire;

為演藝人員祈願文

慈悲偉大的佛陀！
在現代的社會裡，
有一項值得大家重視的職業，
　　那就是演藝人員。

慈悲偉大的佛陀！
我歌頌演藝人員，
　　不是羨慕他們華麗的外表，
　　而是因為他們精湛的演出；
我讚美演藝人員，
　　不是羨慕他們台上的表演，
　　而是因為他們真情的表露。

慈悲偉大的佛陀！
演藝人員為了完美動人的表現，
　　必須承受多少的考驗！
演藝人員為了講究逼真的效果，
　　往往不惜身家性命。
有時必須進出火窟，

Sometimes they must climb cliffs;
Sometimes they must jump from heights;
Sometimes they must dive into the depths of the sea.
They endure the discomfort of wearing stiff costumes
In order to acquaint us with historical figures;
They endure the great burdens of shooting on location
In order for us to appreciate local customs and the sights of different places;
They play contemptible and treacherous characters—
In spite of the upbraiding of audiences—
In order for us to learn the difference between loyalty and disloyalty, between good and evil;
They diligently force themselves to recite their stage dialogue and study all kinds of characters
In order for us to enjoy remarkable authenticity.

Oh great, compassionate Buddha!
Beneath their dazzling external appearances,
Performing artists may have lonely minds;
Beneath their glamorous makeup,
Performing artists may have experienced many hardships.
Some of them struggle to survive
And are forced to rush between rehearsals constantly;
Some of them are bound by contracts

有時必須攀爬岩壁，
有時必須高空翻滾，
有時必須潛入海底。
他們忍受穿古裝的艱苦，
　　讓我們看到歷史人物的神采；
他們忍受拍外景的辛勞，
　　讓我們欣賞各地的風土人情；
他們不顧觀眾的責罵，扮演奸佞的角色，
　　讓我們了解忠奸善惡的辨別；
他們辛苦地強背台詞，揣摩各種的角色，
　　讓我們欣賞維妙維肖的人物。

慈悲偉大的佛陀！
演藝人員在光鮮的表相下，
　　也有一顆孤寂的心靈；
演藝人員在亮麗的化妝下，
　　也有許多辛酸的故事。
他們有的迫於生計，
　　不得不過著軋戲奔忙的日子；
他們有的基於簽約，

And are forced to reluctantly accept unreasonable scripts;
Some of them are under the scrutiny of the public
And lose their privacy;
Some of them pursue fame and fortune,
And lose their direction.
Like Chinese opera singer Mei Lanfang,[4]
Who spread Beijing opera all over the world;
Martial arts director Bruce Lee,[5]
Whose movies were known throughout the world;
Actress Ling Po,[6]
Whose popular Huangmei folk melody brought many people to tears;
Taiwanese opera singer Yang Lihua,[7]
Whose Taiwanese folk opera created a sensation in Southeast Asia.
They have brought esteem to the Chinese people;
They have brought inspiration to their fellow citizens.

Oh great, compassionate Buddha!
May all performing artists
Leave a rich and beautiful legacy
For the performing arts;
May all performing artists
Write a glorious chapter
In the performing arts;

不得不強顏接受無理的劇本；
　他們有的在公眾矚目下，
　失去了自己的隱私；
　他們有的在財貨名利中，
　迷失了自己的方向。
梅蘭芳[4]的京劇弘揚到全世界，
李小龍[5]的功夫片揚名海內外，
凌波[6]的黃梅調賺人多少熱淚，
楊麗花[7]的歌仔戲轟動東南亞，
　他們為中國人帶來了榮耀！
　他們為同胞們帶來了啟示！

慈悲偉大的佛陀！
願演藝人員都能為演藝生涯，
　留下豐美的歷史；
願演藝人員都能為演藝事業，
　寫下輝煌的篇章。

May we all be "faithful to the script";
Even though life is changeable and full of ups and downs,
May we all play our own roles well.

Oh great, compassionate Buddha!
May we all have the spirit of collaboration;
Regardless of who plays the lead and who the supporting role,
We should cooperate with each other
To perform impressively on the stage of life.

Oh great, compassionate Buddha,
Please accept our sincerest prayer!
Oh great, compassionate Buddha,
Please accept our sincerest prayer!

願大家都能有忠於劇本的精神，
　　即使人生起伏多變，
　　也要扮演好自己的角色；

願大家都能有集體創作的精神，
不分主伴，彼此配合，
將人生的舞台演得有聲有色。

慈悲偉大的佛陀！
請求您接受我至誠的祈願。
慈悲偉大的佛陀！
請求您接受我至誠的祈願。

A Prayer for Transportation Industry Professionals

Oh great, compassionate Buddha!
When you contemplate the all-encompassing reach
Of your perception through your wisdom eye,
You have undoubtedly seen
The complicated transportation systems constructed by
        humankind,
And the many routes that sprawl across our lands and seas;
From a distance, they look like cobwebs, or
Like the squares of a chess board.
We would like to express
Our sincere gratitude and respect
For people who work daily in transportation:
For their knowledge and skills in operating these systems
To promote the interaction and flow of culture,
And for their ability to operate these delivery systems
That promote the progress and prosperity of the world.

Oh great, compassionate Buddha!
Through their assistance
We can accomplish the dream
Of having the supernatural power to travel freely
Through the boundless universe to our hearts' content.
When transporting passengers and goods

為交通人員祈願文

慈悲偉大的佛陀！
在您的慧眼遍觀十方時，
可以看到人類繁複的交通系統，
可以看到佈滿海陸的運輸動線，
   它們好像蜘蛛羅網，
   它們如同各式棋盤。
我們要特別對交通勤務人員，
   表示感謝與敬佩。
因為他們善於應用這些交通系統，
   促進了人類的溝通與交流；
因為他們善於應用這些運輸動線，
   促進了世界的進步與繁榮。

慈悲偉大的佛陀！
他們乘載著我們，
   讓大眾實現神足通的願望，
   在大千世界盡情遨遊；
他們順利地將乘客及物品，

From one station to another,
From one city to another,
They enable us to enjoy comfortable and attentive service.

Oh great, compassionate Buddha!
Please look:
The drivers on our roads
Must endure the frustrations of congested traffic,
And remain constantly on guard against the sudden occurrence of accidents;
The steersmen that navigate our seas
Must carefully negotiate fierce winds and surging billows,
And must be skillful in avoiding dangerous shoals and undercurrents;
The pilots in our skies
Must protect the airplanes from the effects of turbulence,
And must adapt to irregular schedules;
Those who are responsible for serving passengers
Must constantly meet the demands of their clients
And maintain their ability to be instantly responsive.
And those who are responsible for directing traffic
Must stand in the middle of the road,
Brave the harshness of the weather,

從這一站送到那一站，
從這一個城市運到那一個城市，
　　讓我們享受舒適週到的服務。

慈悲偉大的佛陀！
請您看！
陸地車輛的駕駛，
　　必須忍耐塞車的辛苦，
　　必須注意突發的事故；
海上船隻的駕駛，
　　必須小心應付暴風惡浪，
　　必須長於躲避暗潮險灘；
空中飛行的駕駛，
　　必須讓機身免於氣流的影響，
　　必須讓自己適應不定的作息。
還有那些交通服務人員，
　　必須時時滿足乘客的需求，
　　必須具有臨時應變的能力；
還有那些交通安全人員，
他們站在馬路中央，
　　不計日曬雨淋，

Suffer the heat, and the odor of pollution,
And withstand the incessant murmur of the traffic;
They endure all fatigue and exhaustion
In order to allow the traffic flow to be safe and smooth,
In order to allow passengers to feel comfortable on the journey.

Oh great, compassionate Buddha!
Thanks to these remarkable professionals,
We are able to smoothly finish conducting our business;
Thanks to these diligent professionals,
We are able to travel all over with peace of mind.

Oh great, compassionate Buddha!
We pray for all transportation industry professionals:
May they value the idea of "safety first";
May they strive for quality in the rendering of service;
May they have the virtue of being patient and gentle;
May they have the temperament of being amiable and kind.
We pray for all travelers:
May they all be able to leave home happily
And return home safely.

不計寒冬溽暑，
　鼻尖吸著蒸騰的廢氣，
　耳邊響著隆隆的車聲；
他們百般勞累，
只為了讓車流平安順暢，只為了讓乘客賓至如歸。

慈悲偉大的佛陀！
因為有了這些優秀的交通人員，
　我們才能順利地將事務辦妥；
因為有了這些勤奮的交通人員，
　我們才能安心地到各地旅遊。

慈悲偉大的佛陀！
我們祈願天下所有的交通人員，
　都能具有安全第一的理念，
　都能具有服務至上的精神，
　都能具有忍耐柔和的雅量，
　都能具有親切和藹的態度。
祈願所有旅行出外的人，都能
　快快樂樂地出門，平平安安地回家。

We pray for those who work daily in transportation:
May they all be able to do their duties happily
And complete their duties safely.

Oh great, compassionate Buddha,
Please accept our sincerest prayer!
Oh great, compassionate Buddha,
Please accept our sincerest prayer!

祈願從事交通勤務的人,都能
　　快快樂樂地工作,平平安安地完成。

慈悲偉大的佛陀!
請求您接受我至誠的祈願,
慈悲偉大的佛陀!
請求您接受我至誠的祈願。

A Prayer for Maritime Professionals

Oh great, compassionate Buddha!
In this world,
The ocean has played a complex role.
She is the compassionate mother of the great earth,
Who fosters the resources of life
And harmonizes the breath of the earth.
She is also a friend to humankind
Who grants convenient and direct navigation routes,
And provides natural protection.
However, she is also imperious, prone to anger,
Stirring up mighty currents and tidal waves at any time;
However, she is also a capricious lady
Who conceals swift currents and perilous shoals.

Therefore,
We would like to express our special gratitude to maritime professionals:
They live in the company of the ocean
Without concern for their own safety,
To safeguard the lives of humankind;
They contend with the ocean,
Without regard for their own lives,
To ensure the safety of the masses.

為海域工作者祈願文

慈悲偉大的佛陀！
在這個世間上，
海洋扮演著複雜的角色：
她是大地的慈母，
　孕育生命的資源，調節地球的呼吸；
她是人類的朋友，
　賜予便捷的航道，提供天然的屏障。
但她也是易怒的君主，
　隨時會掀起巨浪與海嘯；
但她也是善變的女郎，
　不時暗藏著急流和險灘。

因此──
我們要特別感謝海域工作者，
他們不計安危，與海洋為伴，
　維護人類的生存；
他們不顧身命，與海洋周旋，
　保障大眾的安全。

Among these professionals,
Some are officers and people in the navy,
Who defend our nation's territory;
Some are in the coast guard,
To preserve the peace and order of our nation;
Some are sailors in the merchant marine,
Who facilitate transportation;
Some are rescue workers,
Who handle critical emergency situations;
Some are divers
Who explore the sea and search for treasures.

In the vast ocean:
They could be blown overboard by fierce winds;
They could be swept off the deck by swift currents;
They could run aground on hidden reefs;
They could be drowned by ferocious waves.
In these perilous circumstances,
They risk their lives.
Yet for the welfare of humankind,
They accept the challenges of the ocean without ever turning back.

從事海域工作的人員，
有的是捍衛國土的海軍將士，
有的是維持治安的海上警察，
有的是利濟運輸的行船職員，
有的是處理危急的救難英雄，
有的是探險尋寶的潛水人員。

他們在浩瀚的海洋裡，
狂風，可能會將他們吹走；
急流，可能會將他們捲去；
暗礁，可能會讓他們擱淺；
巨浪，可能會把他們淹沒。
在這險惡的環境中，
儘管冒著生命的危險，
他們為了人類的幸福，
　仍義無反顧地迎向海洋的挑戰。

Oh great, compassionate Buddha!
Maritime professionals are great, dedicated champions.
In the sweltering summer weather,
Their skin is exposed, and darkened by the scorching sun;
The soles of their feet are scalded by the searing decks;
In bitterly cold areas,
Their bodies endure bone-piercing chills;
They are surprised by the appearance of menacing icebergs.
In order to accomplish their mission,
They still devote themselves
To the embrace of the ocean without any reservation,
In spite of facing hardships and adversities.

Oh great, compassionate Buddha!
Please enable them to maintain cool calmness
Despite the sweat of summer;
Please enable them to possess warm enthusiasm
Despite the severity of winter.

Oh great, compassionate Buddha!
Maritime professionals, while fulfilling their duties,

慈悲偉大的佛陀！
海域工作者是偉大的堅忍鬥士。
　在溽暑的季節裡，
　　烈日將他們的皮膚曬得黝黑，
　　甲板將他們的腳底燙得發熱；
在嚴寒的區域裡，
　冷風刮削著他們的肌肉骨髓，
　冰山會突然露出猙獰的一面。
儘管面對艱苦困難，
他們為了達成任務，
仍無怨無悔地投入大海的懷抱。

慈悲偉大的佛陀！
請讓他們在涔涔汗水中，
　仍能保持心中的清涼；
請讓他們在風霜雨雪中，
　仍能擁有沸騰的熱血。

慈悲偉大的佛陀！
海域工作者一旦來到海洋，

Must endure the discomfort of motion sickness,
And the loneliness of homesickness.
We sincerely pray for maritime professionals:
May they remain aware
That their families are eagerly awaiting their return;
May they realize
That their relatives and friends are praying for them;
May they sail on the winds
Of confidence always and everywhere;
May they maintain indomitable spirits,
Regardless of safety or danger.

Oh great, compassionate Buddha,
Please accept our sincerest prayer!
Oh great, compassionate Buddha,
Please accept our sincerest prayer!

必須忍耐船上暈眩的痛苦,
必須忍耐船上思鄉的寂寞。
我們深切地祈願海域工作者——
都能了解父母妻兒在倚門而望,
都能知道親朋好友在祝福他們:
希望他們無論何時何地,
都要張滿信心的風帆;
希望他們無論是安是危,
都要鼓舞奮發的鬥志。

慈悲偉大的佛陀!
請求您接受我至誠的祈願,
慈悲偉大的佛陀!
請求您接受我至誠的祈願。

A Prayer for Prostitutes

Oh great, compassionate Buddha!
We would like to share our thoughts with you:
Prostitutes are disparaged by much of society;
But as you may know,
They suffer inhumane treatment, and
They live a hellish life.
Their situation deserves of our sympathy,
And their existence deserves our attention.
The hearts of prostitutes are bleeding
And yet they have to feign a joyous mood.
Every day, prostitutes hope for dawn,
And yet they pass the days as if they were years.

Oh great, compassionate Buddha!
Society and the masses look down on prostitutes,
Considering them to be promiscuous, inconstant, and
　　　　lascivious,
Believing that they sell their bodies and souls,
And corrupt the morals of society.
Actually, among these fragile, weak females:
Some have been abducted by harmful "friends";

為煙花女子祈願文

慈悲偉大的佛陀！
我要向您投訴，
煙花女子是被人輕賤的行業，
但您會知道，
她們受的是非人的待遇，
她們過的是地獄的生活，
她們的處境值得人們可憐，
她們的存在值得人們探討。
那些煙花女子啊！
她們的心在滴血，卻要強顏歡笑。
她們每天冀望黎明，卻在度日如年。

慈悲偉大的佛陀！
社會大眾輕視煙花女子，
認為她們生張熟李，水性楊花；
認為她們出賣靈肉，敗壞風俗；
其實身為弱者的她們，
　有些是被損友拐騙的，

Some have been seduced by immoral people;
Some have been forced to support impoverished families;
Some have been sold by heartless relatives.
Only a few of them enter the profession of their own free will.
Since ancient times, among prostitutes:
There have been talented women
Of outstanding artistic ability;
There have been young women
Of chivalrous spirit and tender thoughts;
There have been loyal and patriotic women;
There have been bodhisattvas protecting and upholding the correct doctrine of Buddhism.
If not for Sai Jinhua[8] during the Boxer Rebellion,[9]
The Invasion of the Eight Powers[10] would never have been stopped;
If Cai Songpo[11] had not had Xiao Fengxian,
Yuan Shikai[12] would have never been overthrown quickly.
Even when you were dwelling in the world, Buddha,
Lady Amra of India donated the Amra Garden[13] to you,
And converted it into a place for propagating the Dharma;
The esteemed Vasumitra[14] liberated all beings to be free
From desires and attain purity through skillful means.
Although life's vicissitudes have been frustrating,
These women still remembered to give joyously to help others;

有些是被歹徒引誘的，
有些是被家庭的困境所逼，
有些是被狠心的親人所賣，
只有極少數的人是自甘墮落。
更何況自古以來，
煙花女子當中，
也有藝能出色的才女，
也有俠骨柔情的紅妝，
也有忠貞愛國的巾幗，
也有護持正法的菩薩。
義和團事件[9]如果沒有賽金花[8]，
八國聯軍[10]那裡會善罷甘休？
蔡松坡[11]如果沒有小鳳仙，
洪憲帝制[12]那裡能順利推翻？
甚至佛陀您住世時，
菴摩羅女捨園[13]為寺，代眾請法；
婆須蜜多[14]權巧方便，度眾離貪。
她們雖然境遇坎坷，卻不忘喜捨助人；

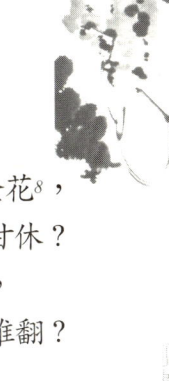

Although they had taken a wrong path into the world of prostitution,
They still upheld their principles.

Oh Buddha!
Prostitutes are often oppressed by immoral people,
And frequently endure beatings;
Prostitutes live under adverse circumstances,
And are often abused, and die unnatural deaths.

Oh great, compassionate Buddha!
We pray for your compassion to pity these poor women:
May they be able to escape from the sea of misery
And find a reputable profession soon;
May they be able to marry without difficulty,
And lead normal lives.

Furthermore,
We hope that, with principles and courage,
Society will assist the police in bringing to justice
These villains who force women into prostitution,
And help these women to escape the torment of their predicament.
May these women be able to regain
Confidence in their respectability;

她們雖然誤入風塵，卻沒有隨波逐流。

佛陀啊！佛陀！
煙花女子在歹徒的監視下，動輒遭到拳打腳踢，
煙花女子在惡劣的環境中，常被蹂躪亡於非命。

慈悲偉大的佛陀！
祈求您慈悲可憐這些煙花女子，
讓她們能脫離苦海，早日轉業，
讓她們能順利從良，正常生活。

更希望社會大眾，都能發揮道德勇氣，
協助警方打擊逼良為娼的惡人；
幫助她們逃出痛苦煎熬的火坑。
讓她們能夠拾回做人的信心，

May they be able to restore
Order and peace to their lives.

Oh great, compassionate Buddha!
Please let all men in the world
Correct their confused perceptions;
Please let all females in the world embody
The dignity of one's mother or sister.

Oh great, compassionate Buddha,
Please accept our sincerest prayer!
Oh great, compassionate Buddha,
Please accept our sincerest prayer!

讓她們能夠重建生活的規律。

慈悲偉大的佛陀！
讓天下的男士能矯正錯亂的觀念，
讓天下的女性有如姐如母的尊嚴。

慈悲偉大的佛陀！
請您接受我至誠的祈願！
慈悲偉大的佛陀！
請您接受我至誠的祈願！

A Prayer for the Drivers of All Vehicles

Oh great, compassionate Buddha!
Please allow us to express our gratitude and respect
To the drivers of all vehicles!

Oh great, compassionate Buddha!
When we are in need of medical assistance
It is they who deliver us to the hospital in time;
When we are busy,
It is they who diligently deliver us to our destination;
When we are visiting friends or traveling,
It is they who skillfully lend us aid;
When we are replenishing stock or delivering goods,
It is they who promptly help us to transport the goods.

Oh great, compassionate Buddha!
Drivers are a group of unsung heroes
Who work hard and make great contributions;
Drivers are people of virtue
Who embody all varieties of skills:

為汽車駕駛祈願文

慈悲偉大的佛陀！
請求您讓我向汽車駕駛員
　　說出我對他們的感謝和敬意！

慈悲偉大的佛陀！
當我們生病受傷的時候，
　　是他們及時地把我們送進醫院裡；
當我們忙碌的時候，
　　是他們認真地將我們送達目的地；
當我們訪友旅行的時候，
　　是他們熟練地為我們服務；
當我們進貨出貨的時候，
　　是他們迅速地幫我們運載。

慈悲偉大的佛陀！
駕駛員是一群勞苦功高的無名英雄，
駕駛員是具備各種條件的有道之士：

They must have not only
Consummate driving skill and experience,
But also a perfectly calm demeanor;
They must not only perform
Careful inspections of their vehicles,
But also obey traffic regulations;
They must not only be familiar
With all routes and connections,
But also keep their vehicles clean;
They must not only endure
The frustrations of congested traffic,
But also prevent accidents;
They cannot run through red lights,
Overload their vehicles, speed, or drive recklessly.
In today's society, with its heavy traffic:
Roads are as dangerous as the mouth of a tiger;
Level ground is as perilous as a pit.
We depend on these professional drivers
To focus on benefiting self and others
So that traffic will be safe and unimpeded ahead.
We hope that all drivers of the world will remember:
"Slow down, slow down, safety first;
"Slow down, slow down, courtesy first;
"Slow down, slow down, respect first;
"Slow down, slow down, peace first!"

他們不但要有嫻熟的駕駛技術，
　　更要有心平氣和的態度；
他們不但要作好車輛檢查，
　　更要遵守交通規則；
他們不但要熟悉各種路線，
　　更要保持車輛整潔；
他們不但要忍耐塞車之苦，
　　更要防備交通事故；
他們不能亂闖紅燈超載超速，
　　更不能橫衝直撞地行車。
在今日交通發達的社會裡，
馬路如虎口，平地如險坑，
交通要靠這些優良的駕駛員們，
發揮自利利他的精神，
　　才能保障安全，才能暢通無阻。
我們希望天下的駕駛員們都能了解：
　　「不急，不急，安全第一；
　　不急，不急，禮讓第一；
　　不急，不急，尊重第一；
　　不急，不急，平安第一！」

We hope that all drivers of the world will remember:
That a willingness to yield may save their lives;
That their families eagerly await their return,
    so they should drive safely;
That they should never drive under the influence of
    intoxicants,
And never drink while driving;
That they should avoid excessive fatigue,
And rest at regular intervals.

Oh great, compassionate Buddha!
The lives of drivers and passengers are connected as one,
There is a close bond between drivers and the masses.
Smooth traffic keeps everyone in convenient reach;
Safe driving keeps everyone in close connection.
Therefore, we should respect each other, and
We should humbly make way for each other.

Oh great, compassionate Buddha!
With your great power,
We pray to you for your blessing and protection:
May all drivers drive without impediment;
May all drivers travel happily and comfortably.

我們希望天下的駕駛員們都能知道：
「讓人一步路，能保百年身；
　妻兒倚門望，安全駕駛歸；
　喝酒不開車，開車不喝酒；
　疲勞不開車，開車要休息。」

慈悲偉大的佛陀！
駕駛與乘客的生命是繫為一體的，
駕駛與大眾的關係是息息相關的。
便利的交通讓每一個人天涯若比鄰，
安全的行駛讓每一個人兩地如一家。
　所以，我們要彼此尊重，
　所以，我們要互相禮讓。

慈悲偉大的佛陀！
祈求在您大力庇護之下，
所有的駕駛員能順利通暢地駕駛，
所有的駕駛員能歡喜自在地來往。

Oh great, compassionate Buddha!
We also pray to you to bless and support all passengers
          and drivers:
May they obey traffic regulations;
May they preserve traffic safety;
"May everyone leave home happily
"And return home peacefully and safely";
May we be an orderly and courteous society;
May we be an ethical and respectable nation.

Oh great, compassionate Buddha,
Please accept our sincerest prayer!
Oh great, compassionate Buddha,
Please accept our sincerest prayer!

慈悲偉大的佛陀！
也祈求您加持所有的乘客與駕駛們，
    都能遵守交通規則，都能維護交通安全；
讓大家都能，
    「快快樂樂的出門，平平安安的回家。」
讓我們成為一個有秩序禮貌的社會，
讓我們成為一個有道德尊嚴的國家。

慈悲偉大的佛陀！
請您接受我至誠的祈願，
慈悲偉大的佛陀！
請您接受我至誠的祈願。

A Prayer for Our Teachers

Oh great, compassionate Buddha!
Today your disciples come before you
To offer gratitude to our teachers:
For it is their efforts, teachings, and guidance
That enable us to gain knowledge and skills;
It is their guidance toward the right path
That enables us to nurture our understanding and wisdom.
We therefore vow to strive forward and progress diligently,
To repay the great dedication
Our teachers have shown in teaching us;
We also vow to do all we can,
And make contributions to society,
To repay our teachers' kindness.

Oh great, compassionate Buddha!
All teachers are like candles:
They radiate light to illuminate students;
All teachers are like lotus flowers:
They emit sweet balm to benefit students;
They regard the achievements of students
As their personal glory;
They regard the contributions of students
As their personal pride;

為教師祈願文

慈悲偉大的佛陀！
今天弟子來到您的座前，
　　特別向您報告我們對老師的感謝。
因為有了他們的辛勞教導，
　　我才能夠獲得學問技能；
因為有了他們的指引誘導，
　　我才能夠長養知識智慧。
我要在此發願：我要努力向上，
我要精進不懈，來報答老師的苦心；
我要盡己之力，我要奉獻社會，
　　來回饋老師的恩德。

慈悲偉大的佛陀！
所有的老師都像蠟燭一樣，
　　燃燒自己，照亮學生；
所有的老師都像蓮花一樣，
　　吐露芬芳，嘉惠學子。

They regard the advancement of students
As their personal joy;
They regard the endeavors of students
As their personal motivation.

Oh great, compassionate Buddha!
How could we possibly begin to repay our teachers
For the great benevolence they have bestowed upon us?
How could we possibly begin to thank our teachers
For their lofty status and exalted teachings?
By praying to you, Buddha, may we
Transfer the merits of all of our accomplishments
To our teachers and parents:
May those who are still alive be at ease,
And all their wishes fulfilled;
May those who are deceased have increased merits,
And be reborn in the land of Amitabha Buddha;
Wherever our teachers and parents are
May they be aware of our insignificant accomplishments,
And be filled with delight and comfort.

他們將學生的成就，看成是自己的榮耀；
他們將學生的貢獻，看成是自己的驕傲；
他們將學生的上進，看成是自己的喜悅；
他們將學生的奮發，看成是自己的動力。

慈悲偉大的佛陀！
請您告訴我：
浩浩師恩，何以為報？
巍巍師道，何以為謝？
只有祈求佛陀您慈悲地允諾我，
如果我有點滴的成就，
請都回向給我的老師與父母，
　　願他們生者一切自在，萬事如意；
　　願他們逝者增添功德，往生佛國。
如果我有些許的作為，
無論老師與父母在天涯海角，
　　希望他們都能夠知道，
　　好讓他們感到欣喜安慰。

Oh great, compassionate Buddha!
Education is the cradle that fosters talent;
Education is the foundation that a society is built upon.
We pray to you to support all teachers with your great power:
May they embody your wise skill
Of adapting instruction to individual abilities;
May they embody your ideal
Of balancing practice and understanding;
May they embody your compassionate model
Of not neglecting anyone;
May they embody your magnanimous power
Of respecting both teachers and students;
May they be able to understand that what all beings need in education:
Is not pieces of knowledge, but a fortress of erudition;
Is not the dried vines of dogma, but the vibrant garden of life;
Is not an elegantly adored appearance, but a profound, internal spirit;
Is not lavish gifts, but the fountain of truth.

Oh great, compassionate Buddha!
Once again, we pray to you to support all teachers with your great power:
May they be able to aspire to nurture the talented;
May they demonstrate the spirit of teaching without weariness.

慈悲偉大的佛陀！
教育是孕育人才的搖籃，
教育是建設社會的根本。
祈求您能加被所有的老師，
讓他們能擁有您觀機逗教的智慧，
讓他們能擁有您行解並重的理念，
讓他們能擁有您不捨一人的慈悲，
讓他們能擁有您師徒同尊的胸襟。
希望他們都能了解：
眾生所需要的教育——
不是知識的瓦礫，而是學問的堡壘；
不是教條的枯藤，而是生命的花園；
不是裝飾的花鬘，而是深邃的內涵；
不是溺愛的禮物，而是真理的泉源。

慈悲偉大的佛陀！
再一次請求您加被所有的老師，
　　讓他們都能擁有作育英才的抱負，
　　讓他們都能實踐誨人不倦的精神。

Through a sound and complete education,
May the talented disperse throughout the world,
May society be fortunate and peaceful.

Oh great, compassionate Buddha,
Please accept our sincerest prayer!
Oh great, compassionate Buddha,
Please accept our sincerest prayer!

祈願在健全的教育下，
　人才能夠廣被天下，社會能夠祥和安樂。

慈悲偉大的佛陀！
請求您接受我至誠的祈願，
慈悲偉大的佛陀！
請求您接受我至誠的祈願。

A Prayer for Mass Communication Professionals

Oh great, compassionate Buddha!
With great excitement, we would like to report to you
The recent advancements in the mass communications industry:
Telecommunications industry professionals
Seem to have the supernatural power of clairaudience;
Televised broadcasting professionals
Seem to have the supernatural power of clairvoyance;
Publishing industry professionals
Seem to have the supernatural power of psychic traveling;
Computer networking professionals
Seem to have the supernatural power of mental telepathy.

Oh great, compassionate Buddha!
Mass communication professionals
Have made glorious achievements in modernization, and
Outstanding contributions toward promoting knowledge;
Mass communication professionals
Have had significant influences on diversity, and
Profound importance in the dissemination of information.
Their achievements entail an influential
And burdensome responsibility;
Their merits and demerits are determined
In a single moment of decision.

為大眾傳播者祈願文

慈悲偉大的佛陀！
我非常興奮地向您報告：
現在的大眾傳播事業——
電訊業者好像有了「天耳通」，
電視業者好像有了「天眼通」，
報章雜誌業者好像有了「神足通」，
電腦網路業者好像有了「他心通」。

慈悲偉大的佛陀！
大眾傳播業者，
　　他們對現代化有輝煌的成就，
　　他們對知識化有卓越的貢獻，
　　他們對多元化有重大的影響，
　　他們對普及化有深遠的意義。
他們的成就，任重道遠，
他們的功過；在一念間。

These remarkable professionals must provide information that:
Is not only objective, detailed, and thoughtful,
But also vivid and interesting;
Is not only disseminated broadly,
But also touches people deeply;
Is not only educational,
But also rich in culture;
Is not only the truth of the matter,
But also promotes the interactions of humanity.

Oh great, compassionate Buddha!
Mass communication professionals are able to promote world peace;
They are able to lend impetus to the progress of civilization.
In this age of information overload,
Humankind relies on benevolent communication professionals
To promote knowledge and ability;
Humankind relies on outstanding communication professionals
To transmit the rich legacy of our culture.

Oh great, compassionate Buddha!
We pray for all professionals in mass communications:
May they all practice professional ethics;
May they all respect others' privacy;
May they all strive to absorb new knowledge;

優秀的大眾傳播業者，
不但要讓資訊客觀詳實，也要讓資訊生動有趣；
不但要讓資訊廣泛傳播，也要讓資訊打動人心；
不但要讓資訊具備教育的功能，
　　也要讓資訊富含文化的價值；
不但要讓資訊表達事實的真相，
　　也要讓資訊促進人類的交流。

慈悲偉大的佛陀！
傳播業者能促進世界的和平，
傳播業者能推動文明的進步。
在今天資訊爆炸的時代裡，
人類要靠善良的傳播業者，提昇良好的智能水準；
人類要靠傑出的傳播業者，傳遞精緻的文化遺產。

慈悲偉大的佛陀！
我們祈願天下的傳播業者——
　　都能具有職業的道德，
　　都能尊重別人的隱私，
　　都能努力地攝取新知，

May they all unceasingly revise their work and bring forth new ideas.

Oh great, compassionate Buddha!
We hope that all professionals in mass communications
Will relay more information about:
The warm and sweet side of the world;
The kind and beautiful side of society;
The bright side of ideas;
The ethical side of life.

Oh great, compassionate Buddha!
Not only do these mass communication professionals
Have the responsibility of relaying information,
They also have the duty to educate people.
They are good teachers and helpful friends to all people;
They urge political improvements in the nation.
We need them to disseminate all new knowledge;
We need them to report every news item;
We need to rely on their analysis of every critical political and economic issue;
We need to rely on them to represent every thought of the average person.
With the support of your estimable power,

都能不斷地改革創新。

慈悲偉大的佛陀！
我們希望所有的從業人員——
　　多報導世間的溫馨面，
　　多報導社會的善美面，
　　多報導思想的光明面，
　　多報導人生的道德面。

慈悲偉大的佛陀！
大眾傳播業者，
不但對社會有傳播的責任，
　　還負有教育群眾的任務。
他們是全民的良師益友，
他們能督促國家政治的進步，
　　一個新知，要他們傳播；
　　一則新聞，要他們報導；
　　重大的政經問題，要靠他們分析；
　　升斗小民的心聲，要靠他們代言。
希望在佛陀您威力加被之下，

We pray that we all are able to obey morality, ethics, and
    good conscience,
And that we all are able to preserve the harmony and happiness
    of our society.
May all humankind become
People of virtue and righteousness;
May the mundane world transform into
The Humanistic Pure Land soon.

Oh great, compassionate Buddha,
Please accept our sincerest prayer!
Oh great, compassionate Buddha,
Please accept our sincerest prayer!

大家都能遵守道德良知,大家都能維護社會和樂,
讓全體人類都能成為諸上善人,
讓娑婆世界早日轉為人間淨土。

慈悲偉大的佛陀!
請求您接受我至誠的祈願,
慈悲偉大的佛陀!
請求您接受我至誠的祈願。

A Prayer for Postal and Cable Service Professionals

Oh great, compassionate Buddha!
With the sincerest intentions, we would like to relate to you
Our gratitude to postal and cable service professionals.
Postal and cable service professionals
Are the messengers of our modern society;
Because of them,
Travelers may alleviate their homesickness;
Because of them,
Lovers may express their inner feelings to each other;
Because of them,
Faraway friends may communicate without impediment;
Because of them,
Businesses may achieve maximum results.
They allow emergencies to receive a timely response,
They allow political and economic affairs to be handled properly.
Like a bridge, they link the friendly sentiments of human relations;
Like a road, they convey the prosperity of society;
Like a boat, they ferry interactions between people;
Like a truck, they bring us untold convenience.

為郵電人員祈願文

慈悲偉大的佛陀！
弟子要以最誠懇的心意向您訴說，
　我們對郵電人員的感謝。
郵電人員是現代社會的傳遞使者，
有了他們，
　離家的遊子可以解除鄉愁；
有了他們，
　相愛的情侶可以互訴衷曲；
有了他們，
　遠方的友人可以來往無礙；
有了他們，
　工商的來往可以事半功倍。
他們讓緊急事故得到及時瞭解，
他們讓政經事務得到妥善處理。
他們如同橋樑，溝通了人際的情誼；
他們如同道路，促進了社會的繁榮；
他們如同舟船，利濟了民眾的交流；
他們如同車乘，代替了大家的腳步。

Oh great, compassionate Buddha!
During war, a letter from home is worth
Ten thousand pieces of gold;
We pray that all postal and cable service professionals in the world
May find honor in their work
And take pride in their important industry.

Oh great, compassionate Buddha!
Please consider this:
In order to deliver the mail, mail carriers
Brave the hardships of severe weather,
And are undaunted by the barking of vicious dogs;
In order to sort out and distribute the mail, postal clerks
Disregard the fatigue clouding their eyes,
And the dullness of repetitive motion;
In order to disseminate information, correspondents
Toil to receive and send dispatches
In spite of minute and detailed inquiries from people;
In order to install cables, electricians
Risk the danger of falling into valleys

慈悲偉大的佛陀！
烽火家書抵萬金，
祈願天下的郵電人員，
　能夠以郵電工作為榮，
　能夠以郵電事業為傲。

慈悲偉大的佛陀！
您看！
郵務士為了運送郵件，
　不計日曬雨淋的辛勞，
　不計惡犬呼呼地吼叫；
分揀員為了撿擇郵件，
　不計眼花撩亂的疲累，
　不計重覆動作的枯燥；
通訊員為了傳遞消息，
　不計收發通訊的辛苦，
　不計民眾查詢的繁瑣；
電技師為了架設電纜，
　不計摔落山谷的風險，

And being struck by lightning or electric shock.
A single, careless, slight error
May affect the operations of an entire plant;
A momentary lapse in caution
May delay the business of an entire region.
When accidents occur
And mail, communications, and power are interrupted,
Postal and cable service professionals
Are the first to receive harsh criticism and unending demands
   for explanations;
Postal and cable service professionals
Must deal promptly with accidents,
Investigate and quickly discover the causes, and rectify
   problems immediately.
Postal and cable services, and the happiness of all people,
Are related as closely as each breath is to the next;
The postal and cable industries
Are closely connected to the advancement of society.

We thus pray to you, Buddha, for your blessings and protection:
May we have the awareness
To be grateful, and cherish things;
May we have the magnanimity
To respect and praise others;
Through mutual cooperation and help,

不計雷霆電擊的危難，
他們一個按鈕不小心，
　也許就會影響全部的運轉；
他們一個環節不留意，
　可能就會耽誤全民的事務。
一旦意外發生，
斷郵、斷訊、斷電的時候，
郵電人員必須首當其衝，
　忍受無情的責怪，回答不停的質問；
郵電人員必須立刻處理，
　趕緊查明原因，及時修補錯誤。
郵電工作和全民的幸福息息相關，
郵電事業和社會的進步密切相聯。

所以更祈求佛陀您的庇祐，
　讓我們有感恩惜福的認識，
　讓我們有尊重讚美的雅量；
希望在彼此互助之下，

May the goal of uniting humanity be realized soon;
May the ideal of a harmonious, equal, and just world be established soon.

Oh great, compassionate Buddha,
Please accept our sincerest prayer!
Oh great, compassionate Buddha,
Please accept our sincerest prayer!

天下一家的目標能早日實現,
大同世界的理想能早日來到。

慈悲偉大的佛陀!
請求您接受我至誠的祈願,
慈悲偉大的佛陀!
請求您接受我至誠的祈願。

A Prayer for Recycling Professionals

Oh great, compassionate Buddha!
We would like to sincerely inform you:
This world is now piled high with wasted resources;
Our earth is plagued with problems resulting from refuse and pollution.
In the past, people often said,
"Every single grain is hard to come by,
"Every single thread is a scarce resource."
People today,
Because of mindless consumption,
Discard things as soon as they get them
And consume wastefully everywhere.
Fortunately, we have recycling professionals
Who silently dedicate themselves:
They remain unperturbed by the hardships of exposure to severe weather;
They risk the dangers of being infected by viruses;
They disregard the fatigue of collecting refuse door-to-door;
They sort all refuse and separate it;
They produce merit in the midst of refuse.

Oh great, compassionate Buddha!
Those who engage in recycling are like strong commanders,

為資源回收者祈願文

慈悲偉大的佛陀！
我誠懇地向您報告：
現在世界上，充斥著資源浪費的現象；
現在地球上，滿載著廢物污染的問題。
過去的人常說：
　一粥一飯，當思來處不易；
　一絲一縷，恆念物力維艱。
現代人卻因為信手拈來，
　隨取隨丟者比比皆是，浪擲物品者處處可見。
幸好有默默付出的資源回收者，
他們不計日曬雨淋的辛苦，
他們迎向氣候冷熱的變化，
他們冒著感染病毒的危險，
他們不顧沿門收集的勞累，
將廢棄物分類整理，在垃圾堆中作功德。

慈悲偉大的佛陀！
從事資源回收的人如同

Turning defeated troops into courageous warriors;
Those who engage in recycling are like compassionate herb doctors,
Concocting a panacea from withered trees and decayed stones;
Those who engage in recycling are like meticulous craftsmen
Forging scrap metal into fine steel;
Those who engage in recycling are like clever homemakers,
Turning leftovers into delicacies.
Through skillfulness and ingenuity
They make use of discarded things;
Through their kindness and benevolence,
They make the useless into usable resources.

Through their toil,
They bring new life to discarded resources;
They extend the usable life of worn-out things;
Through their endeavors,
They diminish the effects on the public of environmental pollution;
They create a beneficial cycle for the ecosystem.

Oh great, compassionate Buddha!
Please support recycling professionals with your great power:

把殘兵敗卒訓練成勇士的統帥，
從事資源回收的人如同
把枯木朽石泡製成仙丹的良醫，
從事資源回收的人如同
把破銅爛鐵鍛鍊成精鋼的名匠，
從事資源回收的人如同
把剩菜殘羹烹煮成佳餚的巧婦。
在他們的巧手慧心下，腐朽轉化為神奇；
在他們的善心美意下，廢物變成了資源。

由於他們的辛勞，
　為廢棄資源賦予嶄新的生命，
　為陳舊物品延長使用的壽命；
由於他們的努力，
　改善了環境污染的公害，
促進了生態良性的循環。

慈悲偉大的佛陀！
祈求您加被資源回收者，

May their efforts receive the recognition they deserve;
May their contributions remain in the minds of people;
May their enthusiasm never wane;
May their dedication become a model for society.

Oh great, compassionate Buddha!
You once said,
"Sentient beings and non-sentient beings
"Have the same perfect knowledge."
Everything is full of the value of life.
We pray for your compassion to support all people.
May they all learn from the example
And diligence of recycling professionals:
Parents should love underachieving children;
Teachers should encourage struggling students;
Supervisors should train inept workers;
Officials should advise under-informed citizens.
We should all emulate the example of recycling professionals,
And treat unfavorable things
As good causes and conditions for cultivating body and mind,
And further transform them into a motivation to excel;
We should all emulate recycling professionals,

讓他們的付出得到更多的肯定，
讓他們的貢獻引起大眾的反省，
讓他們的熱忱能夠保持到永久，
讓他們的精神成為社會的典範。

慈悲偉大的佛陀！
您曾說：「情與無情，同圓種智。」
每一件事物都具有生命的價值。
祈求您慈悲加被所有的人，
讓他們都向資源回收者學習，
父母，不要嫌棄笨拙的兒女；
師長，不要捨棄難教的子弟；
主管，不要氣惱愚昧的屬下；
大官，不要討厭頑愚的民眾。
我們都應該向資源回收者看齊，
將不好的事物，
看成是修身養性的好因緣，
　進而轉化為自我奮發的動能；

And listen to harsh words
As if they are the dharani of all Buddhas and bodhisattvas,
And further transform them into loving-kindness, compassion,
*   joy, and equanimity.*

Oh great, compassionate Buddha,
Please accept our sincerest prayer!
Oh great, compassionate Buddha,
Please accept our sincerest prayer!

將刺耳的語言，
聽成是諸佛菩薩的陀羅尼，
　　進而轉化成慈悲喜捨的願力。

慈悲偉大的佛陀！
請求您接受我至誠的祈願，
慈悲偉大的佛陀！
請求您接受我至誠的祈願。

A Prayer in Honor of Servicepeople Killed in Action

Oh great, compassionate Buddha!
"Harsh winds chill the Yi River;
"The departing warriors may never return."
This is exactly the state of mind
Of servicepeople going to battle;
This is exactly the belief
That servicepeople embrace and uphold.
In order to save the country and its people,
They sacrifice themselves;
Their lives and fiery spirits go down in history as heroic.
In order to complete the mission,
They risk (or even lose) their lives, and engage in
A high-spirited action with bravery and loyalty.
Their fearless and undaunted courage, and wisdom,
Are enough to startle the universe and move all beings;
The courage to heroically sacrifice themselves for their country
Is moving enough to shake the mountains and exhaust the oceans.

Oh great, compassionate Buddha!
Some of these servicepeople sacrificed their lives for the homeland;

為陣亡將士祈願文

慈悲偉大的佛陀！
「風蕭蕭兮易水寒，
　壯士一去兮不復返。」
這正是將士們出征的心情，
這正是將士們抱持的信念。
他們為了救國救民，犧牲小我，
　用生命及熱血，寫下悲壯的歷史；
他們為了完成任務，捨身拚命，
　用奮勇與忠誠，譜出激昂的樂章。
他們視死如歸的膽識，
　足以驚天地，泣鬼神！
他們慷慨赴義的勇氣，
　足以撼山岳，傾江海！

慈悲偉大的佛陀！
　他們為國捐軀了。

Please bless and protect them:
May they be reborn in upper realms;
May they return to the earth by taking vows;
May their bereaved families receive proper care;
May their descendants recount their loyalty and virtues from generation to generation.

Oh great, compassionate Buddha!
What those killed in action
Have left behind for people of future generations
Is far more than their names on tombstones
Or a chapter in our history books;
Although their physical bodies are no longer with us,
The moral fortitude shown in serving their homeland with unreserved loyalty
Will exist as long as the territory of the country and the great earth remain;
Although their physical bodies no longer exist,
Their spirit of sacrifice for the country and the people
Will shine as long as heaven, the earth, the sun, and the moon remain.
The sacrifices of Wen Tianxiang[15] of the Song Dynasty
And Shi Kefa[16] of the Ming Dynasty,
Have been written again and again as poetry,
And praised and extolled by people all over the world;

請求您庇佑他們，
讓他們的忠魂，能夠往生善處，
讓他們的英靈，能夠乘願再來，
讓他們的遺族，得到妥善照顧，
讓他們的子孫，要用忠義傳家。

慈悲偉大的佛陀！
陣亡將士遺留給我們後人的，
　不只是墓碑上的名字，
　不只是歷史上的往事。
他們的肉體雖然已經不在，
　但他們精忠報國的節操，
　卻與山河大地同存；
他們的色身雖然已經消失，
　但他們為國為民的精神，
　將與天地日月同光。
像文天祥[15]、史可法[16]的犧牲，
　一再被寫成詩歌，
　被世人稱頌讚揚；

The loyalty and virtues of Guan Yu[17] in the Epoch of
    the Three Kingdoms,
And Yue Fei[18] of the Song Dynasty,
Have been written again and again as plays,
And admired and appreciated by everyone.
We want to praise and extol
The valor of those who sacrifice their lives for righteousness
And defend their home and the nation;
We want to eulogize their aspirations
To fulfill justice at the cost of their lives, and to quell
    rebellions;
We denounce those invaders
Who expand their territories aggressively, and bring great
    affliction to the people;
We condemn those overly-ambitious people
Who are covetous and selfish.

Oh great, compassionate Buddha!
We pray for your protection:
May all humankind coexist peacefully
And never struggle with each other;
May all sentient beings in all the dharma realms be as one
    family,
And no longer be as incompatible as fire and water.
In the future, may the world:

像關雲長[17]、岳武穆[18]的忠義，
　　一再被編為劇本，
　　被大家讚歎欣賞。
我們要稱揚他們
　　捨身取義，保家衛國的英勇；
我們要謳歌他們
　　殺身成仁，討伐叛逆的雄心；
我們要譴責那些
　　蠶食鯨吞，塗炭生靈的侵略者，
我們要唾棄那些
　　貪婪熾盛，自私自利的野心家。

慈悲偉大的佛陀！
祈求您的覆護，
讓全體人類都能和平共存，
　　不要再互相爭鬥；
讓法界有情都能彼此一家，
　　不要再水火不容。
希望未來的世界，

Have no tyrants who burn, kill, and plunder;
Have no warriors who face each other with vicious weapons;
Have only kind people who are compassionate, and give joyously;
Have only beings who enjoy longevity, peace, and happiness.

Oh great, compassionate Buddha,
Please accept our sincerest prayer!
Oh great, compassionate Buddha,
Please accept our sincerest prayer!

沒有燒殺掠奪的魔王,
沒有凶器相向的武夫;
只有慈悲喜捨的仁者,
只有長壽安樂的眾生。

慈悲偉大的佛陀!
請求您接受我至誠的祈願,
慈悲偉大的佛陀!
請求您接受我至誠的祈願。

A Prayer for Blessings on Our Nation

Oh great, compassionate Buddha!
With the greatest sincerity,
As your disciples,
We are here to express our gratitude for your great protection:
Please let our nation make education available to all;
Please let our people raise their standard of living;
Please let our science and technology continue to improve;
Please let our politics maintain freedom and democracy.

Oh great, compassionate Buddha!
With great sincerity, we would like to express ourselves clearly:
Although education is available to all,
Our ethics have degenerated;
Although our standard of living has been raised,
Our public morality has eroded;
Although our science and technology have advanced,
Our industries have reported frequent incidents of pollution;
Although our political system is democratic,
Our society has been turbulent and ill at ease.

為國家祈福祈願文

慈悲偉大的佛陀！
弟子在這裡
至誠感謝您的加被！
讓我們的國家教育普及；
讓我們的人民所得提高；
讓我們的科技日新月異；
讓我們的政治民主自由。

慈悲偉大的佛陀！
我要向您虔誠發露表白：
雖然我們的教育普及了，
　　但我們的道德卻有淪喪的現象；
雖然我們的所得提高了，
　　但我們的人心反而更加的腐蝕；
雖然我們的科技進步了，
　　但我們的各種工業卻污染頻傳；
雖然我們的政治民主了，
　　但我們的社會卻在動盪與不安！

Oh great, compassionate Buddha!
We thus pray for your great protection:
May the mercilessness and cruelty of our society
Be transformed into harmony and happiness;
May the brazenness and debauchery of our society
Be transformed into proper manners and order;
May the rampancy of crime and misdirection of our society
Be transformed into joyous giving and forming affinity;
May the cheating and imposture of our society
Be transformed into honesty and righteousness;
May the anger, hatred, and jealousy of our society
Be transformed into compassion, kindness, and benevolence;
May the wrong knowledge and wrong views of our society
Be transformed into right knowledge and right view.

Oh great, compassionate Buddha!
We pray for your great support:
May we grasp the concept of cause and effect,
And understand the reality of life;
May we have the strength of a heart full of patience and tolerance,
And never retreat in the face of adversity;
May we be imbued with clear and wise foresight,
And have no fears or worries;
May we have the courage to subdue evils,
And complete the mission of life.

所以，
慈悲偉大的佛陀！
祈願您的加被，
將社會的凶殘暴戾，能轉為祥和歡喜；
將社會的無恥淫亂，能轉為知禮守序；
將社會的豪奪強取，能轉為喜捨結緣；
將社會的騙取詐欺，能轉為誠信有義；
將社會的瞋恨嫉妒，能轉為慈悲仁善；
將社會的邪知邪見，能轉為正知正見！

慈悲偉大的佛陀！
祈願您加持我們，
讓我們擁有因果的觀念，了解生命真相；
讓我們滿懷忍耐的力量，遇挫而不退轉；
讓我們具備明智的遠見，無懼不再煩惱；
讓我們擔當降魔的勇氣，完成人生的使命！

Oh great, compassionate Buddha!
We pray for your blessing and protection:
May our country have favorable weather,
And never have natural disasters or man-made calamities;
May our politics be honest, clean, and just,
And never have corruption or bribery;
May our ethnic groups be tolerant of those who are different,
And never have racial disputes;
May our society be steadfast, prosperous, and powerful,
And never have wars or upheavals;
May our lives be abundant in food and clothing,
And never suffer economic instability;
May our bodies and minds be healthy and carefree,
And never be disturbed by sickness.

Oh great, compassionate Buddha,
Please accept this prayer for our country!
Oh great, compassionate Buddha,
Please accept this prayer for our country!

慈悲偉大的佛陀！
祈求您的庇護，
讓我們的國家風調雨順，永遠沒有天災人禍；
讓我們的政治廉潔清明，永遠沒有貪污賄賂；
讓我們的族群包容異己，永遠沒有種族紛爭；
讓我們的社會安定富強，永遠沒有戰爭暴亂；
讓我們的生活豐衣足食，永遠沒有經濟風暴；
讓我們的身心健康無憂，永遠沒有疾病困擾。

慈悲偉大的佛陀！
請您接受我為國家的祈願！
慈悲偉大的佛陀！
請您接受我為國家的祈願！

A Prayer for World Peace

Oh great, compassionate Buddha!
As your students and followers,
We are sincerely kneeling here before you;
Please listen to these words from our hearts.
The rumbling of war between nations,
The clamor of discord between people,
The roar of greed in the rapids of craving,
The growl of hatred among races.
These sounds are
Like tidal waves storming against our hearts!
These sounds are
Like hurricanes pounding against our hearts!
As we observe all of this,
We realize that all human suffering
Originates from our self-conceit, prejudice, and delusion.
As we contemplate all of this,
We realize that all worldly turmoil
Is caused by our attachment to things, Dharma, and
　　　　relationships.
Disagreement between different people
Has caused so many arguments;

為世界和平祈願文

慈悲偉大的佛陀！
我虔誠地跪在您座前，
請您垂聽我向您訴說心事，
國際間的戰火發出隆隆的炮聲，
人我間的口舌發出惡毒的罵聲，
欲望裡的洪流洶湧澎湃的翻滾，
族群中的仇恨生生不息的蔓延。
那些聲浪啊！
　如排山倒海般的湧來；
那些聲浪啊！
　如淒風苦雨般的襲到！
我張開雙眼仔細觀察，
了解到人間的苦惱重重，
　肇因於我見、人見、眾生見；
我開啟心扉靜靜思維，
體悟到世界的風雲多變，
　起源於事執、法執、人我執。
人際之間的黨同伐異，

Discrimination between different races
Has caused so many disasters;
Intolerance between different religions
Has caused so many misfortunes;
Conflict of interests between different nations
Has caused so much chaos and upheaval.
Living in this kind of world,
Every day we live in fear, with no ease;
Every day we live in senselessness, with no peace.

Oh great, compassionate Buddha!
Please listen to our sincerest prayer.
We sincerely wish that, in this world, there be:
No jealousy, only admiration;
No hatred, only harmony;
No greed, only generosity;
No harm, only achievement.

Oh great, compassionate Buddha!
Let people of different ages
Live in harmony;
Let people of different social stations
Have mutual respect;
Let people of different professions
Work in cooperation;

導致了多少紛爭；
種族之間的歧視凌虐，釀成了多少災難；
宗教之間的排斥傾軋，造成了多少禍患；
國際之間的交相爭利，造成了多少戰亂。
我們生活在這樣的世間上，
　每天在恐怖中不能自在，每天在顛倒中不能安然。

慈悲偉大的佛陀！
　請垂聽我向您祈求的願望：
願這個世界上，
　沒有嫉妒，只有讚歎；沒有瞋恨，只有祥和；
　沒有貪欲，只有喜捨；沒有傷害，只有成就。

讓我們世間上，男女老少都能互相融和；
讓我們世間上，貧富貴賤都能互相尊重；
讓我們世間上，士農工商都能互相合作；

Let people of different religions
Practice with tolerance.

Oh great, compassionate Buddha!
You once said,
"The mind, Buddha, and all sentient beings
"Are no different from one another."
"You, I, and others are all equal."
We need to learn from you the wisdom
To close the distance between self and others;
We need to learn from you the selflessness
To eliminate all of our attachments;
We need to learn from you the truth
To resolve the confrontations between races;
We need to learn from you the compassion
To reconcile the conflicts between nations;
We need to learn from you the Buddha light
To illuminate the darkness of the world.

Oh great, compassionate Buddha!
Please hear my sincere and pious prayer!
Please bestow peace upon the world!
Please bless all sentient beings with harmony!

讓我們世間上，宗教種族都能互相包容。

慈悲偉大的佛陀！
您曾說：
　「心、佛、眾生，三無差別。」
　「你、我、他人，一切平等。」
我們要學習您的智慧，拉近人我間的距離；
我們要學習您的無我，消除眾生們的執著；
我們要學習您的真理，解脫種族中的對立；
我們要學習您的慈悲，化解國際上的干戈；
我們要學習您的佛光，照破世間裡的黑暗。

慈悲偉大的佛陀！
請求您接受我至誠的祈願；
請您給世界和平吧！
請您給眾生安樂吧！

Oh great, compassionate Buddha,
Please accept our sincere prayer!
Oh great, compassionate Buddha,
Please accept our sincere prayer!

慈悲偉大的佛陀！
請求您接受我誠懇的祈願！
慈悲偉大的佛陀！
請求您接受我誠懇的祈願！

A Prayer for Our Natural Environment

Oh great, compassionate Buddha!
We would like to tell you of an unjust situation on our mind:
The world that we live in has been ruined and has fallen ill.
In nature, the mother of this great earth,
Flowers are no longer emitting fragrance;
Birds are no longer singing;
The green mountains are no longer smiling;
The flowing water is no longer crystal-clear.
Please look:
Excessive logging has stripped vast areas of vegetation;
Exhaust pollution has tainted the beautiful and delicate
        appearance of our mountains and rivers;
The once lush forests have now become the houses and
        mansions of people,
Taking away the only sanctuary of many species;
The once crystal-clear lakes have now been polluted
        everywhere;
And the once leaping marine species can now no longer move
        freely.
Our natural resources have been decreasing sharply day by
        day;
How will future generations survive?

為自然生態祈願文

慈悲偉大的佛陀！
我要向您訴說內心不平的現象：
我們居住的地球被摧殘生病了！
自然；這個大地之母，現在已經：
　花不飄香，鳥不歌唱，
　遠山不再含笑，流水不再清澈。
您看！
這裡濫砍爛伐，讓大地的髮絲漸禿漸黃；
那裡廢氣污染，弄髒了山川嬌嫩的容顏。
原本蓊鬱的森林，
　而今都變成人們的洋房豪宅，
　讓鳥獸沒有棲居安身的地方；
原本清澈的湖水，
　現在也到處受到污染，
　原本跳躍的魚蝦，也不再悠遊了。
我們天然的資源日益銳減，
　大家未來的子孫不知如何生存？

The air that we breathe is not clean,
Our health has been threatened.

Oh great, compassionate Buddha!
We have five sense organs: eyes, ears, nose, tongue, and body;
We have five poisons: greed, anger, ignorance, arrogance,
           and doubt;
We are on the verge of destroying our beautiful earth
And disintegrating the ecological relations of nature.
Too many rare birds and animals
Have disappeared into humankind's meals and mouths;
Too many dainties of land and sea
Have gone missing under humankind's guns and knives.

Oh great, compassionate Buddha!
Please let us and our future generations:
Be able to play with fireflies
Under the radiance of star-brimmed skies;
Be able to sing and dance with great nature
On the shore of an emerald sea;
Be able to enjoy fresh air
In the thick forests of towering trees;
And be able to grow together with all things under the sun
On a field that extends out far beyond the horizon.

我們呼吸的空氣已經混濁，
　　人體的健康已經受到威脅。

慈悲偉大的佛陀！
人類的眼、耳、鼻、舌、身五根，
人類的貪、瞋、癡、慢、疑五毒，
　　即將摧毀了美麗的地球，
　　即將瓦解了自然的生態。
多少的珍禽異獸，
　　在人類的碗盤口邊消失了；
多少的山珍海味，
　　在人類的槍聲刀下失蹤了！

慈悲偉大的佛陀！
讓我們和我們的下一代，
能在星斗高掛的夜晚，與螢火蟲一起遊戲；
能在碧波海邊的沙灘，與大自然同歌共舞；
能在參天大樹的密林，享受清新的空氣；
能在一望無際的原野，與萬物共同成長。

This is not just for the natural environment,
But also for the hometowns of humankind;
This is not just for the earth's existence,
But also for our future generations.
Please grant us tender hands
To soothe all sentient beings on earth;
Please grant us ears that listen attentively
To the wondrous sounds of the world and natural phenomena;
Please grant us bright and keen eyes
To discover the limitless treasures of the universe;
Please grant us compassionate hearts
To preserve the ecology of our world.

Oh great, compassionate Buddha!
We can no longer allow mountains and rivers to be tainted;
We can no longer allow the earth to weep;
We can no longer allow living things to be frightened;
We can no longer allow the air to be polluted.
We must strive to let mountains and rivers be splendorous and
　　　　　green again;
We must strive to let the beauty of the earth reappear;
We must strive to restore fragrant, fresh air;
We must strive to let nature become a solemn Pure Land again.

這不只是為了自然生態，而是為了人類自己的家園；
這不只是為了地球生存，而是為了我們未來的子孫。
請您給我們柔軟的手掌，撫慰世間一切的有情；
請您給我們傾聽的雙耳，諦聽自然萬象的天籟；
請您給我們明亮的眼睛，發覺天地無盡的寶藏；
請您給我們慈悲的心意，保護地球寰宇的生態。

慈悲偉大的佛陀！
我們不能再讓山河變色，
我們不能再讓大地嗚咽，
我們不能再讓生物恐懼，
我們不能再讓空氣污染。
我們要努力讓山河再顯蒼翠壯麗，
我們要努力讓大地重現美麗容顏，
我們要努力讓空氣恢復芬芳清新，
我們要努力讓自然回歸莊嚴淨土。

Oh great, compassionate Buddha,
Please accept our heartfelt prayer!
Oh great, compassionate Buddha,
Please accept our heartfelt prayer!

慈悲偉大的佛陀！
懇請您納受我衷心的祈願！
慈悲偉大的佛陀！
懇請您納受我衷心的祈願！

A Prayer for People of All Vocations and Endeavors

Oh great, compassionate Buddha!
We have all devoutly taken refuge in you;
Some of us serve in organizations of industry, commerce, or
    enterprise;
Some work for the institutions of government, education,
    military, or law enforcement;
Some are housewives;
Some are retired, living in well-earned tranquillity.
We often feel the imperfection in ourselves;
We often sense the hardships in our lives.

Oh Buddha, the great one!
We, of all vocations and endeavors,
Are here in front of you today to pray to you.
Oh great Buddha!
We do not ask in hope of enlightenment now;
We pray that you will enable us
To become kind people.
We do not ask in hope to eliminate all worries;
We pray that you will enable us
To have fewer worries.

為社會大眾祈願文

慈悲偉大的佛陀！
我們是一群虔誠皈依您的弟子：
    有的人在工商企業單位服務，
    有的人在公教軍警機關工作，
    有的人是家庭主婦，
    有的人已退休閒居。
我們經常覺得自己不夠完美，
我們時時感到人生苦難頻繁。

佛陀！偉大的佛陀！
今天我們各界人等齊聚在您座前，
    為的是想向您祈願：
偉大的佛陀！
要我們人人成佛，我們不敢有此奢求，
不過，我們所要祈求的，
是讓我們能成為好人；
要我們斷盡煩惱，我們不敢奢望達到，
但是，我們所要祈求的，是讓我們少煩少惱。

Oh great, compassionate Buddha!
Through the guiding light of your compassion,
May our laborers, through diligent effort:
Apply themselves, increase production,
And bestow great contributions upon our nation;
May our farmers strive to:
Produce bountiful harvests, increase variety,
And ensure that people never lack the basic necessities;
May our business sector:
Further promote research and development, seek profitable returns on investments,
And provide numerous conveniences for the community;
May teachers:
Guide and protect their pupils, foster talent through education,
And elevate society to brighter and vaster horizons;
May parents:
Raise their children with love, abide honestly by principles,
And establish fine models for future generations.

Oh great, compassionate Buddha!
We pray that we, and people of every social status,
Through the nurture and protection of your immeasurable kindness,
May all follow the Triple Gem faithfully,

慈悲偉大的佛陀！
仰仗您的慈光庇照，
讓我們的勞工能努力工作，
　增加生產，為國家作出最大的貢獻；
讓我們的農夫能勤於耕種，
　改良品種，使民眾免於衣食的匱乏；
讓我們的商家能研究發展，
　將本求利，為人群提供最大的方便；
讓我們的教師能愛護子弟，
　作育英才，使社會擁有無窮的希望；
讓我們的父母能慈愛子女，
　誠實守道，為後輩樹立良好的模範。

慈悲偉大的佛陀！
希望我們所有的人等，
在您慈雲覆護之下，
　人人謹守三皈，奉行五戒；

Uphold the five precepts;
Devote ourselves to eliminating all wrongdoings,
Strive to do good;
Have deep understanding of the law of cause and effect,
Repent our karmic hindrances;
Cultivate positive affinity with others,
And benefit society.

Oh great, compassionate Buddha!
Through the great assistance of your wisdom,
We pray that we, and people of every vocation and endeavor,
May cultivate ourselves in speech and thoughts,
Set ourselves right and help others reform;
Strengthen the bonds among relatives and others,
Bring harmony to our families and order to our nation;
Understand the principle of dependent origination,
Realize the truths of interdependence and coexistence;
Carry out the teachings of the Noble Eightfold Path,
And live a normal life.

Oh great, compassionate Buddha!
We sincerely reveal our hearts to you.
We pray that you aid all people in the world
To eliminate greed, anger, and ignorance,
And to diligently cultivate precepts, meditation, and wisdom.

人人盡心去惡，努力行善；
人人深信因果，懺悔業障；
人人廣結善緣，福利社會。

慈悲偉大的佛陀！
希望我們各行各業，
在您的慧日庇照之下，
　每一個人都能修口修心，正己正人；
　每一個人都能敦親睦鄰，齊家治國；
　每一個人都能懂得緣起真理，相互依存；
　每一個人都能奉行八正道法，正常生活。

慈悲偉大的佛陀！
我們將自己的心聲虔誠上達於您，
祈求您能加持全世界的人類，
　息滅貪瞋愚癡，勤求戒定智慧；

We pray that you encourage all sentient beings in the universe
To learn respect and tolerance,
And to live in consummate harmony, without dispute.

Oh great, compassionate Buddha,
Please hear our sincere and pious prayer!
Oh great, compassionate Buddha,
Please hear our sincere and pious prayer!

祈求您能促進全法界的眾生，
　學習尊重包容，彼此和合無諍。

慈悲偉大的佛陀！
請您接受我們至誠懇切的祈願，
慈悲偉大的佛陀！
請您接受我們至誠懇切的祈願！

A Prayer for Victims and Families of the September 11th Disaster

Oh great, compassionate Buddha!
There were disasters in New York City, Washington, D.C., and
    Pittsburgh.
The World Trade Center has collapsed,
And portions of the Pentagon are in ruins.
Have you heard the wailing of the suffering masses?
Have you witnessed the agony of the shattered families?

Oh Buddha!
These are the pleas from a hell on earth!
These are the cries for help from a world calamity!

Oh great, compassionate Buddha!
There,
Buildings and houses have collapsed,
Devastation abounds amidst the wreckage and rubble;
There,
Sand and stones fly all over,
Misery and suffering greet the eye everywhere.

為九一一罹難者祈願文

慈悲偉大的佛陀！
恐怖份子攻擊美國的暴行發生了！
紐約世貿大樓爆炸傾倒，
五角大廈也便成了斷壁殘垣，
您可曾聽到苦難眾生的呼號？
您可曾看到親人離散的慘痛？

佛陀啊！佛陀！
那是人間地獄發出的哀嚎！
那是娑婆浩劫傳出的聲音！

慈悲偉大的佛陀！
那裡，
　天崩地裂，房倒屋毀，
　死傷慘重，觸目驚心；
那裡，
　石爆驚天，火燄四起，
　樓倒人亡，觸目驚心；

So many were trapped in the wreckage, filled with fear;
So many were confined in dangerous places, unable to escape;
So many lost their families in just one morning, with loved ones forever separated;
So many lost their lives, homes, and belongings in a flash.
They were desperate for the relief of the rescue crew!

Oh Buddha!
They are in dire need of your blessing and protection!
They are like lost travelers
Looking for a secure home;
They are like frightened lambs
Seeking a safe shelter.
Some of them tragically fell victim to the disaster;
Some of them were innocently wounded and disabled.

Oh great, compassionate Buddha!
We pray for your blessings:
May the survivors be relieved of their suffering
And recover their good health;
May the deceased be reborn
In the Pure Land of Amitabha Buddha.

多少人身陷災區中，日夜恐慌；
多少人困在危地裡，無法出離；
在瞬息間，骨肉離散，天人永隔；
在剎那間，家園全毀，財物盡失。
他們多麼需要救難人員及時來到！

他們多麼需要佛陀您加持與庇護！
他們那時像迷失的遊子，
　　都在尋找寄住的家園；
他們那時像驚惶的羔羊，
　　都在尋覓安全的依怙。
他們有的不幸罹難了，他們有的無辜傷殘了。

慈悲偉大的佛陀！
祈求您的加被
讓他們生者消災免難，健康如昔；
讓他們亡者往生佛國，蓮登九品。

Oh great, compassionate Buddha!
May they realize that all physical homes
Go through the stages of formation, abiding, decay, and extinction,
That only their self-nature can sustain forever;
May they all understand that death and separation
From family and loved ones befalls all of us,
That only enlightenment and liberation are our ultimate security.

Oh great, compassionate Buddha!
Please bless and protect the survivors of these disasters:
Please grant them the confidence to live a new life,
May they know that where there is life there is hope;
Please grant them the courage to move on,
May they understand that where there is survival there is strength.

Oh great, compassionate Buddha!
Please give them your blessings,
That their bodies and minds may heal quickly;
Please give them the strength of equanimity,
That their painfully sad spirits may regain joyfulness.
Please let them understand

慈悲偉大的佛陀！
請求您讓他們都能體悟，
　　現實的家園會有成住壞空，
　　自己的本性才能永恆安住；
請求您讓他們都能了解，
　　即使骨肉至親，也會有生離死別，
　　只有證悟解脫，才是究竟的依靠。

慈悲偉大的佛陀！
請求您庇佑劫後餘生的人們，
賜給他們再生的信心，
　　讓他們知道：活著就有希望；
賜給他們向前的勇氣，
　　讓他們明白：生存就是力量。

慈悲偉大的佛陀！
請您給他們福佑，
　　讓他們身心的創傷趕快轉危為安；
請您給他們定力，
　　讓他們悲痛的情緒得到轉苦為樂。
請求您讓他們明白，

*That only through rebuilding their own lives with fresh energy
Can they enable the deceased to obtain the greatest consolation
And can they themselves obtain the ultimate success.
Furthermore,
We pray that this disaster will not worsen, and
That such disasters will never occur again.
Please bless and support all people:
May we all realize that the lives of self and others are interconnected;
May we all understand that we all affect each other in our relationships.
We must take preventative measures in time of peace,
We must cooperate with and help each other,
And be prepared for possible future perils, while enjoying peace.*

*Oh great, compassionate Buddha,
Please accept our sincerest prayer!
Oh great, compassionate Buddha,
Please accept our sincerest prayer!*

唯有振作精神，重整家園，
才能讓亡者得到最大的安慰，
才能讓自己得到最後的成功。
我們更祈求，
這次的災情不要再擴大，
類似的禍害不要再發生。
更祈求您加被所有的民眾，
讓大家都知道你我生命是共通的，
讓大家都體會自他關係是互動的；
我們一定要在平時作好防範工作，
我們必須要互助合作，居安思危。

慈悲偉大的佛陀！
請求您接受我至誠的祈願，
慈悲偉大的佛陀！
請求您接受我至誠的祈願。

A Prayer To Respectfully Welcome a Relic of the Buddha's Tooth

Oh great, compassionate Buddha!
Thank you!
The relic of a tooth of your true body has finally come to Taiwan.
It is you who gives us faith;
It is you who gives us glory;
It is you who gives us Truth;
It is you who gives us support.

Oh great, compassionate Buddha!
We would like to confess to you:
We often have confusion and distress in our lives;
We frequently are unable to be completely and thoroughly thoughtful in conducting ourselves and handling affairs.
We need to rely on your instruction to avoid suffering;
We need to follow your guidance to be happy and blissful.

From now on:
We vow to follow your teachings;
We vow to exalt your Truth.

恭迎佛牙祈願文

慈悲偉大的佛陀！
感謝您！
您的真身佛牙舍利終於降臨台灣了。
　是您，給我們信心；
　是您，給我們榮耀；
　是您，給我們真理；
　是您，給我們依靠。

慈悲偉大的佛陀！
我們要向您發露：
　我們每日生活常常會有妄心煩惱，
　我們做人處事往往不能圓滿周到，
　我們要仰仗您的開示，讓大家都能免除痛苦。
　我們要遵循您的教導，讓大家都能幸福美好。

從今天起，
　我們誓願奉行您的遺教，
　我們誓願發揚您的真理。

Oh great, compassionate Buddha!
Please support us with your power:
From this day forward,
May we all carry out the "Three Goods"—
Saying good words, doing good things, and having good intentions.
May we pursue the "Three Studies"—
Upholding pure precepts, cultivating meditative concentration, and increasing wisdom.
May we eliminate the "Three Poisons" in life—
Abstaining from greedy desires, getting rid of anger, and removing ignorance.

Oh great, compassionate Buddha!
Our families lack true affection,
Our society's morals are corrupted,
Our people have jealous and narrow minds, and
Our world is in turmoil and danger.
We hope that you will give us all faith and hope,
We hope that you will elevate our morals:
From now on, may our minds be kind and bright,
From now on, may our world be friendly and peaceful,

慈悲偉大的佛陀！
請加被我們，從今天起，
讓我們全民都能做到「三好」，
　　說好話，做好事，存好心。
我們要實踐您的「三學」，
　　持淨戒，修禪定，學智慧。
我們要去除人生「三毒」，
　　戒貪欲，去瞋恨，除邪見。

慈悲偉大的佛陀！
　　我們的家庭缺乏真愛，
　　我們的社會風氣敗壞，
　　我們的人心褊狹嫉妒，
　　我們的世界動亂危害。
希望您給我們全民信心希望，
希望您提昇我們的道德人格；
　　讓我們的人心從此善良光明，
　　讓我們的世界從此友愛和平，

May our people embody correct knowledge and views, and
May our country be wealthy and peaceful.

Oh great compassionate Buddha!
From this day forward,
We want to experience and realize
The truth of dependent origination that you discovered.
From this day forward,
We want to follow the five precepts and the ten wholesome
　　　conducts that you promoted:
Not to violate the safety of others,
Not to take the wealth of others,
Not to slander the reputation of others, and
Not to destroy the good deeds of others.

Oh great, compassionate Buddha!
We want to understand facts and principles clearly,
We want to strive forward,
We want to vow to help others, and
We want to endeavor to make some contributions to society.

Oh great, compassionate Buddha!
We pray in front of the relic of your tooth,
That you will display the light of your wisdom to its fullest,
That you will manifest your respect-inspiring virtue,

讓我們的人民具足正知正見，
讓我們的國家從此富強康樂。

慈悲偉大的佛陀！
從今天起，
我們要體證您發現的緣起真理，
從今天起，
我們要遵循您倡導的五戒十善，
　不侵犯別人的安全，不佔奪別人的財富，
　不毀謗別人的名譽，不破壞別人的好事。

佛陀！慈悲偉大的佛陀！
　我們要明白事理，我們要奮發向上，
　我們要發心成就別人的因緣，
　我們要努力對社會有所貢獻。

佛陀！慈悲偉大的佛陀！
祈求您的佛牙舍利，
　發揮您的慧光，顯現您的威德，

That you will grant us wisdom and compassion, and
That you will grant us faith and strength,
So that our tomorrow will be better
And our future more wonderful.

Oh great, compassionate Buddha,
Please accept the prayer that we say on behalf of the masses!
Oh great, compassionate Buddha,
Please accept the prayer that we say on behalf of the masses!

賜予我們智慧慈悲,賜予我們信仰力量,
　讓我們明天會更好,讓我們未來更美妙。

慈悲偉大的佛陀!
請您接受我代大眾所作的祈願。
慈悲偉大的佛陀!
請您接受我代大眾所作的祈願。

A Prayer for the Buddha's Birthday

Oh great, compassionate Buddha!
We are here to celebrate with sincerity and respect
Your birth into this world.
When all the flowers bloomed during the warmth of spring,
Exotic flowers were contending in beauty and fascination in
    the Lumbini garden;
Everyone in Kapilavatthu was rejoicing,
Gentle breezes spread the fragrance,
All birds sang in unison;
From that moment on,
There was promise in the human world,
From that moment on,
There was Dharma in the human world.

With one hand pointing to the sky
And the other pointing to the earth,
You declared that you were
The uniquely honored one in the world.
As you took seven steps,
Clusters of lotus flowers appeared,
And you used the pure and clean Dharma water
To wash away the stains of the earth.

佛誕節祈願文

慈悲偉大的佛陀！
  我們在此地虔誠恭敬地禮拜，
  因為您誕生到世間來了。
在春暖花開的時候，
  藍毘尼園裡奇葩爭妍，
  迦毘羅衛國中萬眾歡騰，
  和風吹拂芳香，
  眾鳥齊聲歌唱，
  從此人間有了光明，
  從此人間有了佛法。

您一手指天，一手指地，
發出天上天下，唯我獨尊的宣言。
您腳踏七步，蓮花朵朵，
  用清淨法水洗滌娑婆塵土。

Immediately,
Muddy mountain streams became crystal clear,
Burned-out torches were rekindled,
The heavens played wonderful music,
The earth displayed rare, auspicious signs;
All these portents welcomed your arrival to this world.

Oh great, compassionate Buddha!
Because of your birth in this world,
Your forty-nine years of teaching the Dharma
Will hold sway for far more than three great kalpas!
The more-than-three-hundred gatherings in which you taught
   the sutras
Will benefit more-than-countless sentient beings!

Oh great, compassionate Buddha!
It was you who broke the caste system,
You who preached the doctrine of dependent origination and
   the equality of all beings,
You who opened all beings' minds to the Buddha's wisdom
   and views,
You who awakened all sentient beings from ignorance.

Oh great, compassionate Buddha!
In order to receive respectfully the joyous occasion
Of your birth to the world,

頓時，
　渾濁的溪水變得清澈，燃盡的薪火熾盛起來，
　天空奏著優美的音樂，地上出現稀有的瑞相，
這些都是在歡迎聖者您光臨世間。

慈悲偉大的佛陀！
由於您降誕在娑婆世界，
四十九年的說法，
　何止影響三大阿僧祇劫！
三百餘會的談經，
　何止百千萬億眾生蒙福！

慈悲偉大的佛陀！
　是您，打破世間階級的制度，
　是您，宣說緣起平等的法門，
　是您，開示眾生佛陀的知見，
　是您，喚醒廣大有情的沉迷。

佛陀！慈悲偉大的佛陀！
恭逢您降誕在娑婆世界，

In some places, people decorate with lanterns and colored hangings,
Full of joyful atmosphere;
In some places, people hold parades,
And the sounds of gongs and drums shake the sky;
Monasteries hold the ceremony of bathing
The image of the Buddha, as
Devotees and their families celebrate your birthday.
This is how your followers commemorate
Your gracious kindness!
This is how your followers remember
Your blessing and protection with gratitude!

Oh great, compassionate Buddha!
Please sympathize with the imperfections of our virtues and merits;
We can only chant your great, sacred name mindfully,
As though remembering our own kind mother.

Oh great, compassionate Buddha!
We kneel before you,
We pass our hands over your golden body,
We offer our sincere devotion, and

有的地方張燈結綵，
　　喜氣洋洋；
有的地方民眾巡行，
　　鑼鼓喧天；
寺院舉行浴佛典禮，
信徒全家慶祝佛誕。
　這是佛子們在紀念您的恩德！
　這是佛子們在感念您的福佑！

啊！偉大的佛陀！
請悲憫我福薄德淺，
　　只能以思念慈母的心情，
　　稱念您偉大的聖號。

慈悲偉大的佛陀！
　我用雙膝跪在您的座下，
　我用雙手撫摸您的金身，
　我奉上心香一瓣，

We pray and hope that your virtue brightens the world.
May the Dharma last forever.
Please allow our vision to correspond with yours,
And clearly see and understand the suffering of all beings;
Please allow our speech to correspond to yours,
And delight in saying wonderful and kind words;
Please allow our actions to correspond to yours,
By being willing to help our friends;
Please allow our thoughts to correspond to yours,
And concentrate on benefiting all beings.

Oh great, compassionate Buddha!
We offer our entire lives to expound and propagate the Truth;
We offer our entire lives to liberate all sentient beings.

Oh great, compassionate Buddha,
Please accept our sincere prayer!
Oh great, compassionate Buddha,
Please accept our sincere prayer!

祝禱您佛德增輝，法輪常轉。
讓我與您的佛眼相應，洞察眾生之苦；
讓我與您的佛口相應，樂說妙善之語；
讓我與您的佛身相應，常做不請之友；
讓我與您的佛心相應，多行利生之事。

慈悲偉大的佛陀！
　我們願盡形壽，闡揚真理；
　我們願獻身命，廣度有情。

慈悲偉大的佛陀！
請您接受我至誠的祈願，
慈悲偉大的佛陀！
請您接受我至誠的祈願。

A Prayer for the Consecration of a Newly-Completed Statue of Buddha

Oh great, compassionate Buddha!
In our monastery today,
We are holding a ceremony to consecrate
A newly-completed statue of the Buddha.
An assembly of your disciples gathers before you
To praise you sincerely:
"In the heaven above and the earth below,
"There is no one like you, Buddha;
"In the worlds of all directions
"There is no one comparable to you;
"We have seen everything the world has,
"Yet nothing is like you."

Oh Buddha!
We see you sitting straight and proper
On the precious throne of the golden lotus in absolute stillness;
We see your kind and peaceful face and appearance.
We are also mindful of
Your loving-kindness, compassion, joy, and equanimity,
Your supernatural power, your peaceful mind, and your
　　　　Dharma-body
That spreads out over the ten directions without hindrance.

佛像開光祈願文

慈悲偉大的佛陀！
今天是本寺聖像金容的開光典禮，
四眾弟子們都雲集在您的座前，
虔誠地向您讚頌：
　「天上天下無如佛，
　　十方世界亦無比，
　　世間所有我盡見，
　　一切無有如佛者。」

我們看到佛陀您，
　端坐金蓮寶座，如如不動；
我們看到佛陀您，
　容顏和藹安詳，清淨莊嚴。
我們也觀照到佛陀您，
　慈悲喜捨，神通自在；
　法身無礙，遍布十方。

Oh great, compassionate Buddha!
Your kind eyes look at the suffering of all beings with concern,
Your two ears listen to the revelation of all beings with attentiveness,
Your two hands comfort the wounds of all beings, and
Your Dharma voice liberates the minds of all beings.

Oh great, compassionate Buddha!
On your precious altar,
Please accept the offering of our minds
And the offerings of fragrant flowers.
We pray for your support and blessing:
Please let the monastery be ever-more successful
In promoting the Dharma and benefiting all beings;
Please let devotees open their minds and liberate their thoughts
Upon worshipping, and hearing the Dharma.

Oh great, compassionate Buddha!
Your sacred statue has been contributed,
And is supported wholeheartedly, by many devotees.
Oh Buddha, we pray that you bless and protect them:
May they be healthy physically and happy spiritually;
May their careers be free from trouble and from want;
May their families be peaceful and safe,

慈悲偉大的佛陀！
　您的慈眼垂視眾生的苦痛，
　您的雙耳善聽眾生的傾訴，
　您的雙手撫平眾生的創傷，
　您的法音救度眾生的心靈。

慈悲偉大的佛陀！
請您安坐在寶殿上，
　接受我們的心意供養，
　接受我們的香花獻禮。
請您護持加被，
　讓常住在弘法利生中，日漸昌隆，
　讓信者在聞法禮敬下，心開意解。

慈悲偉大的佛陀！
您的聖像金容是由許多信者贊助，
　全心全意的奉獻。
希望佛陀您保佑他們，身體健康，精神愉快；
希望佛陀您保佑他們，事業順利，不虞匱乏；
希望佛陀您保佑他們，家人平安，所求如意；

And may everything turn out as they wish;
May their families be harmonious,
And protect and uphold Buddhism;
May their friends help each other,
And obtain good affinity.

Oh great, compassionate Buddha!
We further pray that everywhere
Within the reach of this monastery:
The sick and the indisposed will
Gain your blessing and protection, and restore their health;
The physically-challenged will
Obtain your support, and relief from suffering;
Women, children, and the weak will
Obtain your great protection and assistance to increase their
    strength;
The victims of disasters will
Obtain your wisdom to overcome their crises.

Oh great, compassionate Buddha!
We pray that you will dwell in everyone's heart:
May everyone always follow Buddhism,
And may everything be peaceful, safe, and auspicious;
May everyone always cultivate merit and wisdom,
And may their lives be free from resistance and care.
We pray, under your great shelter,

希望佛陀您保佑他們，眷屬和諧，護持佛法；
希望佛陀您保佑他們，朋友相助，獲得善緣。

慈悲偉大的佛陀！
我們更希望本道場因緣所及之地，
凡生病違和者，
　　能獲得您的護佑，恢復健康；
凡身體殘障者，
　　能獲得您的加持，減少痛苦；
凡婦孺弱小者，
　　能獲得您的庇照，增加力量；
凡遭受災難者，
　　能獲得您的智慧，衝破難關。

慈悲偉大的佛陀！
願您活在每一個人的心中，
讓大家常隨佛學，事事平安吉祥；
讓大家常修福慧，生活自在無憂。
祈求在您的庇蔭之下，

That those who protect the Dharma will have
Everything turn out to be auspicious and as they wish,
Without any hindrance;
That our monastery will preach the Dharma
And radiate the Buddha's light to shine everywhere;
That our nation and communities will have
Favorable weather and abundance, and live in plenty;
That the world and humankind will be
Harmonious and joyful, respectful and tolerant.

Oh great, compassionate Buddha,
Please accept our sincerest prayer!
Oh great, compassionate Buddha,
Please accept our sincerest prayer!

護法信眾能吉祥如意，一切無礙；
本寺道場能法輪常轉，佛日增輝；
國家社稷能風調雨順，民豐物阜；
世界人類能融和歡喜，尊重包容。

慈悲偉大的佛陀！
請您接受我至誠的祈願，
慈悲偉大的佛陀！
請您接受我至誠的祈願。

A Prayer for Taking Refuge in the Triple Gem

Oh great, compassionate Buddha!
Today is a joyous day for me:
I am no longer lingering on the wrong path;
I am no longer holding on to unwholesome thoughts;
I am becoming your true disciple.
Oh Buddha! Thank you for bringing me
Out of the darkness to this promising world;
Oh Buddha! Thank you for bringing me
Out of the tumultuous world to this monastery;
Oh Buddha! Thank you for bringing me
Out of confusion and attachment to your enlightened teachings;
Oh Buddha! Thank you for bringing me
Away from worries to this pure land of liberation.

Oh Buddha!
You open your arms and lead me to the door of Truth.
Today I kneel before you to take refuge in the Triple Gem:
I vow to commit myself to the Buddha and never rely
On devas, on demons, or on other faiths;
I vow to commit myself to the Dharma and never rely
On the varied teachings of other faiths;
I vow to commit myself to the Sangha and never follow the
    disciples of other faiths.

皈依三寶祈願文

慈悲偉大的佛陀！
今天是我歡喜的日子，
    我不再徘徊於迷途上了，
    我不再執著於邪思中了，
    我要真正地做您佛陀的弟子。
感謝佛陀您把我從黑暗裡帶到光明的世界裡來，
感謝佛陀您把我從染濁裡帶到清淨的道場裡來，
感謝佛陀您把我從迷執裡帶到正覺的佛法裡來，
感謝佛陀您把我從煩惱裡帶到解脫的淨土裡來。

佛陀！是您——
    展開雙手牽引我進入真理之門，
今日在您的座下，皈依三寶——
我誓願皈依佛，從此不皈依外道邪魔；
我誓願皈依法，從此不皈依外道邪教；
我誓願皈依僧，從此不跟隨外道門徒；

In the tumultuous ocean of suffering, the Triple Gem is the rescue boat;
In the blazing house, the Triple Gem is the benefiting rain;
In the dark night, the Triple Gem is the illuminating light;
In the uncertain forked road, the Triple Gem is the guiding compass.

Oh great, compassionate Buddha!
I pray to you:
May I realize the truth of Buddhism;
May I learn the Dharma zealously;
May I recognize my own responsibilities;
May I vow to protect and uphold the Dharma.

Oh great, compassionate Buddha! I pray to you,
Please support me with your power:
As for my family,
I should be concerned and take care of them;
As for the world,
I should have the virtue of gratitude.

Oh great, compassionate Buddha! I pray to you,
May I be neither discouraged nor resentful
When I am defeated and distressed;
May I reflect, be ashamed, and repent
When I am subject to criticism;

滔滔苦海內，三寶為舟航，
燄燄火宅中，三寶為雨澤，
冥冥黑夜裡，三寶為燈燭，
茫茫歧途上，三寶為指南。

祈求您！
慈悲偉大的佛陀！
讓我能了知佛教的真理，讓我能精進地學習佛法，
讓我能認識自己的責任，讓我能發心地護持佛法。

祈求您，偉大的佛陀！
請您加持我，對家人，我要有關懷的照顧；
請您加持我，對世間，我要有感恩的美德。

祈求您，慈悲偉大的佛陀！
讓我在挫敗困厄的時候，能夠不氣不餒不惱；
讓我在遭受批評的時候，能夠反省慚愧懺悔；

May I strive and advance steadfastly
When I encounter an obstacle;
May I be free from worries and suffering
When I am anxious and in fear.

Oh great, compassionate Buddha!
I am very honored to be able to become your disciple;
I will no longer be reborn in the lower realms of the cycle.
I firmly believe that faith will naturally bring the protection
      and support of heavenly beings,
That I will have good causes and conditions, and
That I will encounter benevolent people and good deeds.

Oh great, compassionate Buddha!
From this moment on, I know:
That I am a Buddhist disciple;
That I should understand cause and effect and karmic
      retribution;
That I should realize suffering, emptiness, and
      impermanence;
That I should follow Mahayana Buddhism
And liberate self and others;
That I should cultivate meditation and disciplined conduct
And enlighten self and others.

讓我在遇到瓶頸的時候，能夠積極奮鬥進取；
讓我在恐懼徬徨的時候，能夠無憂無慮無苦。

慈悲偉大的佛陀！
我很榮幸能成為大聖佛陀您的弟子，
我不會再於惡道裡輪迴流轉了，
我堅持信仰自有龍天的護持，
我會擁有好因好緣，我會遇到好人好事。

慈悲偉大的佛陀！
從今而後，
　　我知道我是三寶弟子，
　　我應該要懂得因緣果報，
　　我應該要明白苦空無常，
　　我應該要奉行大乘佛法，自度度他！
　　我應該要修持禪淨戒行，自覺覺人！

Oh great, compassionate Buddha,
Please accept my pious prayer!
Oh great, compassionate Buddha,
Please accept my pious prayer!

慈悲偉大的佛陀!
請求您接受我衷心的祈願,
慈悲偉大的佛陀!
請求您接受我衷心的祈願。

A Prayer for Receiving and Upholding the Five Precepts

Oh great, compassionate Buddha!
We ignorant and distressed beings
Indulge in misdeeds of body, speech, and mind every day,
And let greed, anger, and ignorance run wild.
We are proud, and exalt ourselves like a mountain;
Our jealousy and unwholesome minds are like poison.

Oh great, compassionate Buddha!
If I do not tend to myself and put myself in order,
I will soon be crushed among the masses of society;
If I do not correct and purify myself,
I will soon be drowned in the ocean of samsara.

Oh great Buddha!
Please allow me to turn over a new leaf.
Oh great Buddha!
From this moment on, I am determined
Not to harm others' lives;
From this moment on, I am determined
Not to steal others' property;
From this moment on, I am determined

受持五戒祈願文

慈悲偉大的佛陀！
我們煩惱無明的眾生，
　　每日放縱身口意業，一任貪瞋愚癡橫行，
　　貢高我慢如山，嫉妒惡心如毒。

慈悲偉大的佛陀！
我再不管理自己，整頓自己，
　　我就快要在社會人群中毀滅了！
我再不修正自己，淨化自己，
　　我就快要在生死大海中淹沒了！

偉大的佛陀！
　　請您讓我重新做人吧！
偉大的佛陀！
我決心從今以後，
　　不再殺害別人的生命；
我決心從今以後，

Not to infringe upon others' moral and bodily integrity;
From this moment on, I am determined
Not to impugn others' reputations;
From this moment on, I am determined
Not to indulge in intoxicants.

Oh great Buddha, I pray to you:
May I engrave the resolve to receive the precepts in my heart,
And so, life after life, never violate the precepts again;
May I apply the merits from receiving the precepts,
And so, life after life, meet good Dharma friends.

Oh great Buddha, I pray to you:
Through my ways of treating people,
May I experience the Dharma;
Through worries, cares, and ignorance,
May I develop bodhi.

Oh great, compassionate Buddha!
I will carry out the admonition
"Do no evil, do all good" with determination;

不再盜取他人的財物；
我決心從今以後，
　　不再侵犯他人的名節；
我決心從今以後，不再攻訐別人的名譽；
我決心從今以後，不再吸食害人的毒物。

祈求您！偉大的佛陀！
讓我銘記受戒初心，生生世世不再重犯禁戒；
願我以此受戒功德，生生世世值遇大善知識。

祈求您！偉大的佛陀！
　讓我從待人接物中去體驗佛法，
　讓我從煩惱無明中去開發菩提。

慈悲偉大的佛陀！
我要決心地奉行，
　　諸惡莫作，眾善奉行；

I will achieve the goal
"Resolve and vow for enlightenment,
"Remove unwholesomeness to reveal virtue" with courage.
From now on,
I will transform all my suffering
Into advancement to a higher stage;
I will convert all my tears
Into a resource for cultivation.

Oh Buddha, I pray to you:
From today on,
May I learn not to be greedy,
And be content with a moral life;
May I learn not to be angry,
And reflect on my own flaws;
May I learn not to be ignorant,
And cherish the innate Buddha Nature;
May I learn not to be suspicious or jealous,
And appreciate others' strengths;
May I be as magnanimous as the ocean,
And tolerate worldly disputes;
May I be as humble as the earth,
And tolerate both purity and filth.

我要勇敢地做到，發心立願袪邪顯正。
從今以後，
我要將所受的痛苦，都轉為逆增上緣；
我要將所流的眼淚，都化為修道資糧。

祈求您，佛陀！
從今以後，
讓我學習不貪欲，安於修道的生活；
讓我學習不瞋怒，反省自我的缺陋；
讓我學習不愚昧，珍惜本具的佛性；
讓我學習不疑嫉，欣賞別人的長處；
願我寬容如海，涵容人間的風波；
願我謙卑如地，負載所有的淨穢。

Oh great, compassionate Buddha!
Please listen to me,
Your disciple, who is receiving the precepts,
Today, kneeling before you:
I make this promise, without resentment or regret;
I vow with perfect willingness.

Oh great, compassionate Buddha,
Please accept my sincerest prayer!
Oh great, compassionate Buddha,
Please accept my sincerest prayer!

慈悲偉大的佛陀！
請聽我受戒的弟子，
今日跪在您的座下，
　無怨無悔地作出承諾，
　心甘情願地發出誓言。

慈悲偉大的佛陀！
請求您接受我至誠的祈願，
慈悲偉大的佛陀！
請求您接受我至誠的祈願。

A Prayer for the Offering of Light

Oh great, compassionate Buddha!
Please accept the offering of the lamp of our minds;
In ancient times, humankind moved forward
From a primitive state through the discovery of fire;
Thereafter, a thousand-year-old dark room could be instantly brightened
By the lighting of a lamp;
Ships navigating in the night could identify directions
By signals from a lighthouse;
Pedestrians in dark alleys could walk without fear
By the illumination of street lights.
Light is indeed very important!
However, the tens of thousands of lights in this world
Cannot compare to even a small fraction of yours!
For only the Buddha's light can add brightness to this gloomy world,
Only the lamp of the Dharma can illuminate confused minds.
Your appearance in this world
To reveal the Dharma and benefit us with joy
Has lit the light of Truth;
From that moment on,
All beings in the sea of suffering have the hope of being rescued;

獻燈祈願文

慈悲偉大的佛陀！
　請您接受我呈獻的一盞心燈，
遠古的人類因發明火炬而走出洪荒，
千年的暗室因點亮油燈而頓生光明，
夜航的船隻因燈塔照亮而認清方向，
暗巷的行人因路燈照明而產生勇氣。
燈，實在是太重要了！
　然而世間上千萬盞的燈光，
　都不及佛陀您的千萬分之一，
因為晦暗的世界，
　唯有佛日才能增輝；
因為迷矇的人心，
　唯有法燈才能照亮。
由於您降誕於世間，示教利喜，
　點亮了真理的明燈，
從此，
苦海裡的眾生有了得度的希望，

All sentient beings in the world have joyously obtained the prospect of being liberated.
Many people have freed themselves from the prison of sorrow;
Many people have escaped the flaming house of torment.

Oh great, compassionate Buddha!
The lamp of our minds that we offer to you now
Has no form or image;
It is the torch illuminated
From our Dharma-body and the life of wisdom;
It is the state of mind ignited
From our all-embracing Dharma-body.
We pray for your blessings, Buddha:
May the lamp of our minds
Illuminate all of the numerous worlds;
May the light of our hearts
Bless and protect all sentient beings:
For this lamp is our suchness and Buddha Nature,
For this lamp is our Dharma-body and the life of wisdom.

Oh great, compassionate Buddha!
Much indebted to your prophecy,
The light offered by the poor woman Nanda

婆婆界的有情喜獲得救的未來；
多少人從痛苦的牢籠中解脫，
多少人從熱惱的火宅中超拔。

慈悲偉大的佛陀！
我現在奉獻給您的心燈，
　　無形無相，
它是從我法身慧命裡點亮的火炬，
它是從我法身真如裡燃燒的心情。
希望能夠得到佛陀您的加持，
祈求我這盞心燈，
　　能夠照徹恆河沙數的世界，
　　能夠庇護三界九有的眾生。
因為，
　　這盞燈是我的真如自性，
　　這盞燈是我的法身慧命。

慈悲偉大的佛陀！
難陀女所布施的貧女一燈，

Enabled her to attain Buddhahood
And become the future Dipamkara Buddha;
The eternal light on Mount Hiei[19] in Japan
Has continued to shine all these years.
We would like to express this clearly to you, Buddha,
That today we are here to offer this lamp not for ourselves,
But in the hope that everyone
Will have a bright, glorious future,
In the hope that everyone
Someday will attain Buddhahood together.
Again, we would like to pray for your support, Buddha:
May this light of ours be transformed
Into countless lights that shine on each other
To light up our hope for a better tomorrow for humankind.

Oh great, compassionate Buddha!
In this world,
There are people who need you to grant them
The light to turn over a new leaf;
There are people who need you to grant them
The light to self-examine and reflect;
There are people who need you to grant them
The light of honesty and trust;
There are people who need you to grant them
The light of faith and fortitude.

承蒙您為她授記：
　將來成佛的名號為燈光如來；
比叡山[19]上的不滅之燈，
　多少年來也一直燃放著光明。
我要向佛陀您表白，
今天我奉獻此燈，不為自求，
　只希望大家都有光明燦爛的未來，
　只希望大家都有共成佛道的一日。
我要再一次祈求佛陀您的加被，
讓我這盞燈能夠化為無盡燈，燈燈相映，
　為人類點燃明日的希望。

慈悲偉大的佛陀！
在這個世界裡，
還有許多人需要您賜給他們回頭轉身的明燈；
還有許多人需要您賜給他們反觀自省的明燈；
還有許多人需要您賜給他們敦厚誠信的明燈；
還有許多人需要您賜給他們信心堅強的明燈。
這些都祈求您的慈光加被，
　讓大家都能早日點亮心靈的明燈，

They are all praying for the blessing of your light of compassion.
May everyone ignite the light of the heart soon;
May everyone discover the true Buddha Nature;
May everyone shine on each other and benefit each other;
May everyone shine on forever into the boundless future.

Oh great, compassionate Buddha,
Please accept our sincerest prayer!
Oh great, compassionate Buddha,
Please accept our sincerest prayer!

讓大家都能及時找到自我的本性。
希望大家都能光光相照，彼此互惠；
希望大家都能燈燈相續，盡未來際。

慈悲偉大的佛陀！
請求您接受我至誠的祈願。
慈悲偉大的佛陀！
請求您接受我至誠的祈願。

A Prayer for Those Who Are Becoming Monastics

Oh great, compassionate Buddha!
Today, your disciple _____ , and others,
Shave off their hair and officially enter the monastery.
In order to seek the Truth and practice great filial piety with
    all their might,
They give up what they treasure
And bid farewell to their families;
In order to reach the Pure Land and bravely enter the Way,
They give up all that is difficult
For ordinary people to give up.
We are here, in an incomparable, joyous state of mind,
Kneeling before you to pray:
Please help them to hold fast to their vow
Until the end of all time.

From now on,
The basic skills and the basic knowledge
About different positions required in the monastic life
Will be the lessons that they must learn;
The three thousand and eight thousand forms
Of Buddhist manner
Will be the conditions that they must acquire.

為出家修道者祈願文

慈悲偉大的佛陀！
今天，您的弟子○○等剃除鬚髮，
　　他們，正式加入僧團了。
他們割愛辭親，為求真理而力行大孝；
他們難捨能捨，為登淨域而勇敢入道。
我在此以無比歡欣的心情，
　　長跪在您的座前，
請加被他們盡未來際，
　　發心永不退轉。

從今以後，
三刀六槌、四十八單，
　　將是他們必學的課業，
三千威儀、八萬細行，
　　將是他們必要的條件。

Oh great, compassionate Buddha!
We pray for your great protection:
In the great smelting furnace,
May they forge firm willpower,
And achieve the power of the vow of the mind of Bodhi;
In following the summons of the bell in the morning and the drum in the evening,
May they progress zealously in the five daily sessions of practice,
And foster an auspicious and harmonious temperament;
In accompanying the cloud-shaped, instructional gong and commands,
May they be diligent in all duties and gain lasting growth;
May the monastic assembly
Never abandon responsibility toward the human world;
May all those who renounce
Never forget the welfare of all beings;
May the outstanding members of the Sangha
Bring their strengths fully into play:
Some lecture and teach to establish the foundation of education;
Some edit and write to propagate the Dharma;
Some dwell in foreign lands and teach sentient beings with skillful means;
Some engage in charity and help the sick and distressed.
Sariputra, one of the elder disciples of Sakyamuni,

慈悲偉大的佛陀！
　請求您慈悲加被，
讓他們在大冶洪爐裡，
　鍛鍊堅強的意志，
　成就菩提道心的願力；
讓他們隨著晨鐘暮鼓，
　精進於五堂功課，
　孕育莊嚴祥和的氣質；
讓他們伴著雲板號令，
　勤勞於各種作務，
　獲得千錘百鍊的成長。
願出家的僧眾們不放棄人間的責任，
願所有的入道者不忘記眾生的福祉。
希望僧伽龍象們都能發揮所長，
　有的講課教學，教育紮根；
　有的編輯寫作，文化弘法；
　有的住持一方，方便度眾；
　有的慈善救濟，扶助疾苦。
舍利弗長老監督講堂建設，

Supervised the construction of lecture halls;
Dravya, another disciple of Sakyamuni,
Arranged accommodations for traveling monastics;
Chan Master Baizhang,[20] a noted Tang abbot,
Cultivated the land and attended to daily duties;
Venerable Daoxuan,[21] a celebrated Tang master of the rules
    of discipline,
Translated sutras and wrote;
Master Xuanzang, the famous Tang pilgrim,
Crossed the perilous deserts to India to study and collect
    Buddhist sutras;
Master Jianzhen,[22] a famous Tang monk,
Preached the Dharma in Japan, in spite of his old age and ill
    health.
They all contributed and diffused their lives
In boundless time and space
In hopes that Buddhism would thrive.

Oh great, compassionate Buddha!
Please let all monastics
Follow in the footsteps of ancient virtuous and wise ones,
To quiet the body and mind;
With the six points of reverent harmony,
To broadly enlighten sentient beings;
With the four means of embracing,
To liberate all sentient beings.

陀羅驃尊者負責安排掛單，
百丈禪師[20]農耕、作務，
道宣律師[21]譯經、著述。
玄奘大師橫渡流沙，天竺取經；
鑑真大師[22]老病之軀，東瀛傳教。
他們拋灑生命於無限的時空中，
　　他們只希望佛法能夠興隆。

慈悲偉大的佛陀！
祈求您讓所有的出家修道者，
　　都能追隨古德前賢的腳步，
　　以六和敬安住身心，
　　以四攝法廣度有情。
他們在修道的過程中，

During the process of their cultivation,
Perhaps they will encounter the trial of mundane desires;
During their journey of preaching the Dharma,
Perhaps they will meet with the hindrances of troublesome adversity.
We pray to you, Buddha, to protect them:
May they strengthen their minds that seek enlightenment;
May they contribute and sacrifice;
May they endure what is difficult
For ordinary people to endure;
May they carry out what is difficult
For ordinary people to carry out.
From now on, following their examples,
We are willing to be messengers
Who protect and uphold Buddhism,
And let this clear stream continue unceasingly;
We are willing to be guardians
Who protect Buddhism,
And let this bright lamp be passed down endlessly.

Oh great, compassionate Buddha,
Please accept our sincerest prayer!
Oh great, compassionate Buddha,
Please accept our sincerest prayer!

　或許會遇到塵緣的考驗；
他們在弘法的旅途中，
　或許會遭逢魔難的障礙；
祈求佛陀您能庇佑他們，
堅固自己的道心，
　犧牲奉獻，奉獻犧牲；
　難忍能忍，難行能行。
自今爾後，
我們願作護持的使者，
　讓這一股清流源源不斷；
我們願作衛教的韋陀，
　讓這一盞明燈相傳不盡。

慈悲偉大的佛陀！
請求您接受我至誠的祈願。
慈悲偉大的佛陀！
請求您接受我至誠的祈願。

A Prayer for Devotees

Oh great, compassionate Buddha!
You once said:
Rare and fortunate it is to hear the Dharma;
Rare and fortunate it is to initiate a benevolent mind;
Rare and fortunate it is to be born in a land of religious freedom;
Rare and fortunate it is to be born as human beings.
How honored we feel to be Buddhists!
Today we would like to pray to you on behalf of devotees:
May all devotees follow your teachings;
May we all believe strongly in cause and effect,
And uphold the five precepts;
May we all be devoted to our parents,
And dedicated to our children;
May we all show love and respect as good siblings do,
And respect our spouses;
May we all encourage each other as friends do,
And be open-hearted towards our superiors and subordinates;
May the living Dharma
Be present in both body and mind;
May the humanistic Dharma
Govern our families and manage our careers.

Oh great, compassionate Buddha!
Pious devotees are like a clear stream in the world;

為在家信眾祈願文

慈悲偉大的佛陀！
您曾說過：
　「佛法難聞，善心難發，
　　國中難生，人身難得。」
身為佛子，我們感到多麼榮幸！
今天我要為在家信眾向您祈願：
希望信眾都能依照您的教誨，
　深信因果，奉持五戒，
　孝順父母，教養兒女，
　兄友弟恭，夫妻互敬，
　朋友相勉，上下寬諒。
讓生活的佛法能內外一如，
讓人間的佛法能齊家治業。

慈悲偉大的佛陀！
虔誠的信眾有如紅塵中的清流，

Some of them write diligently,
And preach the Dharma through writing;
Some of them put their eloquence to use,
And help to propagate Buddhism;
Some of them donate money,
And devote their efforts to endowing monasteries;
Some of them offer their bodies and minds
To benefit all beings.

Like Sudatta, the well-known benefactor of orphans and the homeless,
Who built lecture halls for monastics and preached the Dharma;
Like Vimalakirti, the celebrated lay disciple of Sakyamuni,
Who preached the Mahayana Dharma far and wide;
Like Srimala, daughter of the Indian king Prasenajit,
Who revealed the treasury of truth in the palace and converted the whole nation to Buddhism;
Like Yuye, daughter-in-law of Sudatta,
Who made offerings of the four monastic necessities, and respected the Triple Gem.
They had correct knowledge, right views, and moral fortitude,
And were capable of great achievements;
They cultivated body and speech
And purified their minds and thoughts;
They focused on one teacher and one Way,
From beginning to end;

他們有的勤於著作，筆耕弘法；
他們有的出廣長舌，助佛宣化；
他們有的出錢出力，莊嚴道場；
他們有的身心供養，利濟群生。

像須達長者建立講堂，安僧辦道；
像維摩大士四處說法，弘揚大乘；
像勝鬘夫人宮中開示，佛化全國；
像玉耶女子四事供養，恭敬三寶。
他們正知正見，
　有為有守；
他們修身修口，
　淨心淨意；
他們一師一道，
　全始全終；
他們捨身捨命，

They risked their lives to protect Buddhism and the Sangha.
Pei Xiu,[23] a prime minister in the Tang Dynasty,
Who composed and wrote,
And saved Buddhism from misfortune;
Yang Renshan,[24] a pivotal person
Who revived Buddhism in the Qing Dynasty,
Printed sutras, built schools, and propagated the Dharma
    through culture and education;
Lu Bicheng,[25] skilled in many languages,
Who organized and promoted the protection of all lives,
And preached Buddhism to Europe and the Americas;
Sun Qingyang,[26]
Who traveled extensively to protect the Dharma and the Sangha.
They have left a lifetime legacy;
They have left good affinity for all beings;
They have left models of virtue;
They have left resolute hearts for Buddhism.

Oh great, compassionate Buddha!
We would like to pray for all devotees.
May they emulate wise people of the past:
To cultivate the three studies,
To promote the six paramitas,
To attach equal importance to both action and understanding,
To practice the cultivation of both merit and wisdom.

護教護僧。
裴休[23]宰相撰文著述，
　　挽救法難；
仁山[24]居士印經興學，
　　文教弘法；
呂碧城[25]宣揚護生，
　　歐美傳教；
孫清揚[26]四處奔走，
　　護法衛僧。
他們為生命留下了歷史，
他們為眾生留下了善緣，
他們為自己留下了功德，
他們為佛教留下了願心。

慈悲偉大的佛陀！
我要為在家信眾祈願，
希望他們能效法前賢的風範，
　　應該修持三無漏學，
　　應該發揚六波羅蜜，
　　應該注重行解並重，
　　應該實踐福慧雙修。

In the process of initiating their vow,
They may meet with many trials;
On the road to their belief,
They may encounter many adversities.

Oh, Buddha, all of these pitfalls
Require the support of your power:
Please help the devotees to strengthen
The thought that seeks enlightenment;
Please help the devotees to break through
The junctures of great difficulty;
Please let wind, frost, rain, and snow
Turn into enriching nourishment;
Please let conditions that resist advancement to a higher
　　stage
Turn into a resource for the cultivation of the Dharma.

Furthermore, we pray for your great protection:
May the devotees be free from worries, and attain
　　equanimity;
May the devotees achieve bodhi and bring benefits to the
　　world;
May the Sangha and the devotees
Join hands and advance together to propagate Buddhism;
May the Sangha and the devotees
Help and cooperate with each other to create a pure land.

他們在發心的過程中，或許會遇到許多考驗；
他們在信仰的道路上，或許會遭逢許多困境。

這些都要祈求佛陀您的加被，
　　幫助他們堅固道念，
　　幫助他們衝破難關；
讓風霜雨雪轉為滋養的肥料，
讓逆增上緣化為修道的資糧。

更祈求佛陀您的庇佑，
　　讓他們遠離煩惱，現證安樂；
　　讓他們成就菩提，造福世間；
　　讓僧信們攜手並進，弘揚佛教；
　　讓僧信們互助合作，共創淨土。

Oh great, compassionate Buddha,
Please accept our sincerest prayer!
Oh great, compassionate Buddha,
Please accept our sincerest prayer!

慈悲偉大的佛陀！
請求您接受我至誠的祈願，
慈悲偉大的佛陀！
請求您接受我至誠的祈願。

A Prayer for People Who Build and Support Schools

Oh great, compassionate Buddha!
You are the greatest teacher in the world!
By observing the capability of all beings in order to teach them accordingly,
You have helped many to achieve the state of arhat,
And have cultivated many kind bodhisattvas;
By providing education to all people without discrimination,
You have initiated the education of the masses,
And established the six points of reverent harmony in the Sangha.

The famous monastery, Nalanda, in India,
Was the first university to become world-renowned;
Nagarjuna Bodhisattva, the creator of the Madhyamika School,
Was once the president of the university;
Master Xuanzang, the famous pilgrim to India,
Once studied there.
Chinese monasteries have also served
The function of propagating the Dharma.

Oh great, compassionate Buddha!
In an extremely joyous mood, we would like to tell you that:

為興學功德主祈願文

慈悲偉大的佛陀！
您是世界上最偉大的導師，
由於您的觀機逗教，
　　成就了多少大阿羅漢，培養了多少發心菩薩；
由於您的有教無類，
　　開創了平民教育的先河，成立了六種和敬的僧團。

印度那爛陀寺，
　　是舉世聞名的第一所大學，
　　龍樹菩薩曾擔任校長，
　　玄奘大師曾在此求學；
中國叢林也具有傳教的功能。

慈悲偉大的佛陀！
我要以無比歡喜的心情告訴您，

Our scenic, bright, and beautiful Fo Guang University,
Our management-specialized Nan Hua University,
Our grand, American-based Hsi Lai University, and
Our different worldwide Buddhist colleges—
All have beautiful campuses,
All have complete facilities,
All have fine faculties,
All have diligent students.
All this is the result of millions of people who support our schools.
All this is due to the contributions of people who vow to do meritorious work.
We hope that teachers in the colleges and universities
Will gradually influence and lead students patiently on the right path;
We hope that students in the colleges and universities
Will respect teachers and their teachings, and learn tirelessly.
We hope that the relationships between teachers and students in the school
Will be harmonious;
That, with time, the school will progress both within and without,
That the campus will be filled with warm language, and
That classrooms will overflow with an atmosphere of diligent study.

我們風光明媚的佛光大學、
我們管理專長的南華大學、
我們雄踞美洲的西來大學、
我們世界各地的叢林學院，
　它們有典雅的校園，
　它們有完善的設備，
　它們有優良的師資，
　它們有勤奮的學生。
這一切都是百萬人興學的成果，
這一切都是功德主發心的奉獻。
我們希望大學的師長們，
　都能循循善誘，春風化雨；
我們希望大學的同學們，
　都能尊師重道，好學不倦。
希望學校的師生都能水乳交融，
希望學校的內外都能與時俱進，
希望校園裡充滿了溫馨的語言，
希望教室裡盪漾著勤讀的氣氛。

May the people who vow to do meritorious work fulfill their wishes:
Let the university become the model for intellectuals;
Let the university become the "imperial school" for disseminating truth;
Let the university become the cradle for cultivating great people;
Let the university become the place to educate and mold the virtuous and wise.
We hope that our universities
Will become key places for international culture and education,
We hope that our universities
Will become centers for world academic culture.

Oh great, compassionate Buddha!
Further, we hope that the university will be heir to ancient sages
And the teacher of posterity,
And we hope that the university will shoulder the responsibility
Of civilizing the masses through education.
We must uphold the significance of human ideas;
We must uphold the spirit of open-mindedness;
We must uphold the ideal of cultivating merits and wisdom;

願功德主的發心能夠圓成希望——
　　讓大學成為知識份子的典範，
　　讓大學成為傳播真理的黌宮，
　　讓大學成為培養偉人的搖籃，
　　讓大學成為陶鑄聖賢的道場。
希望我們的大學，
　　能成為國際文教的重鎮，
希望我們的大學，
　　能成為世界學術的中心。

慈悲偉大的佛陀！
我們更希望大學能夠擔當
　　承先啟後的使命；
我們更希望大學能夠肩負
　　教化大眾的責任；
我們應該有人文思想的內涵，
我們應該有兼容並蓄的精神，
我們應該有福慧雙修的理念，

We must uphold the training that emphasizes both behavior
    and ideas.

Oh great, compassionate Buddha!
We pray to you to give your great support
To those who offer their mental abilities
To these universities, in response to the Buddha;
May everything turn out as they wish.
We pray to you to protect
Those who, through meritorious works,
Contribute financially and physically to build these
    universities:
May their merits and wisdom be advanced;
May they be peaceful, safe, and fortunate.
We hope that the fund-raising committee
And those who contribute and rejoice
In the building of the university
Will have what they wish for life after life;
May they leave virtue and wisdom to their descendants.

Oh great, compassionate Buddha,
Please accept our sincerest prayers!
Oh great, compassionate Buddha,
Please accept our sincerest prayers!

我們應該有行解並重的教育。

慈悲偉大的佛陀！
祈求您，
加持為大學奉獻心力的有緣人，
    讓他們生活安康，闔家如意；
祈求您，
覆護為大學出錢出力的功德主，
    讓他們福慧增上，平安吉祥；
希望勸募委員及隨喜功德者，
    都能生生世世，所求遂願，
    都能功德智慧，留給子孫。

慈悲偉大的佛陀！
請求您接受我至誠的祈願。
慈悲偉大的佛陀！
請求您接受我至誠的祈願。

A Prayer for a Buddhist Wedding Ceremony

Oh great, compassionate Buddha!
Today, Mr. _____ and Miss _____
Stand before you with sincerity and respect,
Intending to become husband and wife.
We bless this couple:
Under the blessing and protection
Of your compassionate Buddha light,
May they conclude a happy bond as husband and wife;
May they become a Buddhist couple.

They have decided to pray
For your blessings
In forming a new family,
Because they have found that they are well-matched,
And are both of one mind.
A home is a haven where people seek security,
A home is a nest where people obtain warmth.

Oh Buddha! Please bless this couple.
Under the same roof:
May they be respectful of each other;
May they be tolerant of each other;

佛化婚禮祈願文

慈悲偉大的佛陀！
今天虔誠恭敬站在您座前的
○○先生
○○小姐
　他們要結為夫婦了。
我們祝福這一對璧人，
在佛陀您慈光庇照之下，
　締結美滿的姻緣，成為菩提的眷屬。

他們因為
　彼此心心相印，雙雙情投意合，
所以他們決定祈求佛陀您的賜福，
　今後要組織一個新的家庭。
家，是人的避風港，
家，是愛的溫暖窩。

希望佛陀您能庇佑這一對新人，
在同一個屋簷下——
　彼此尊重，相互包容，

May they be understanding of each other;
May they be helpful to each other;
May they be loving to each other all their lives;
May they be together to the end of their lives.

Oh Buddha! Please protect this couple with your power:
In living together, may they
Be devoted to their parents;
Be respectful of their elders;
Be in harmony with their neighbors;
Be enthusiastic in promoting public welfare;
May they be kind to, and love, each other;
May they be compassionate and affectionate.

Oh great, compassionate Buddha!
We hope that the groom will:
Be a hero who protects his wife and children;
Be a gentleman who is honest and faithful;
Be a volunteer who renders services and contributes;
Be a husband who is completely dedicated.
We hope that the bride will:
Be a benevolent person who is enthusiastic in promoting
　　　　public welfare;
Be a teacher who teaches people with skillfulness;

彼此體諒，相互幫助，
讓他們恩愛一生，讓他們白頭偕老。

希望佛陀您能加被這一對新人，
在共同生活中——
　能夠孝順父母，能夠尊敬長輩，
　能夠和睦鄰里，能夠熱心公益，
　讓他們相親相愛，讓他們多情多義。

慈悲偉大的佛陀！
希望今日的新郎：
　能做一個保護妻女的英雄，
　能做一個誠實忠信的君子，
　能做一個服務奉獻的義工，
　能做一個善盡責任的丈夫。
也希望今日的新娘：
　能做一個熱心公益的善人，
　能做一個方便教化的老師，

Be a woman who is kind, loving, and faithful;
Be a wife who is understanding and appreciative.

Oh great, compassionate Buddha!
We pray to you to bless and protect this couple:
May they establish a happy and blissful home;
May they become a good family.
From now on:
May they handle affairs with wisdom;
May they treat others with respect;
May they cultivate mind and body with virtues;
May they conduct themselves and handle matters with compassion.

Oh great, compassionate Buddha!
Please let this couple observe their vows
And remain loving and faithful to each other.
From this moment on, may they be united in love
And may everything go smoothly;
From this moment on, may they share the same feelings towards each other,
And may they make a harmonious and orderly home.
Day and night,
May their lives be auspicious, and
May everyone rejoice.

能做一個善良慈孝的女人，
能做一個體貼讚美的妻子。

慈悲偉大的佛陀！
祈求您加被這一對新人，
　　建立美滿幸福的家庭，成為善因善緣的眷屬。
希望他們今後，
　　能以智慧處理是非，能以恭敬接待他人，
　　能以道德修養身心，能以慈悲做人處事。

慈悲偉大的佛陀！
讓今天這一對新人，
　　遵守須彌的盟誓，彼此恩愛不渝。
從此並蒂蓮開，事事順利；
從此共命鳥和，宜室宜家。
　　晝夜吉祥，人天歡喜。

Oh great, compassionate Buddha!
Please accept the prayer of these friends
Who are sharing their joy with this newlywed couple!
Please accept the prayer of these friends
Who are sharing their joy with this newlywed couple!

慈悲偉大的佛陀！
請您接受我們與會大眾的祈願吧！
慈悲偉大的佛陀！
請您接受我們與會大眾的祈願吧！

A Prayer for the Dharma Propagators

Oh great, compassionate Buddha!
You came to the realization of the Truth of the universe over 2,600 years ago.
From that time on, the world has had bright hope;
Since then, Buddhism has spread worldwide.
We are grateful for those Dharma propagators who have benefitted all beings:
They are like lighthouses that provide direction for people;
They are like sweet dew that brings purity and coolness to people.

Oh great, compassionate Buddha!
The Dharma propagators
Not only must respectfully uphold the pure precepts,
But also have the compassionate vow of liberating all beings;
Not only must they have great knowledge and cultivation,
But also correct knowledge and right view;
Not only must they have dignified manners,
But also merits, virtues, and an untarnished reputation;
Not only must they have eloquence,
But also honesty and righteousness.

為弘法善知識祈願文

慈悲偉大的佛陀！
您在紀元六百年前證悟宇宙真理，
從那時起，世間有了光明的希望；
直到今天，佛法已經遍傳全世界。
感謝弘法利生的善知識們，
　　他們像燈塔，為人們指引方向；
　　他們像甘霖，為人們帶來清涼。

慈悲偉大的佛陀！
弘法利生的善知識們──
不但要奉持淨戒，更要有度眾悲願；
不但要學養豐富，更要有正知正見；
不但要態度莊重，更要有功德清望；
不但要口才敏捷，更要有古道熱腸。

Oh Buddha! May they follow your steps:
To embody your spirit of exercising
Both compassion and wisdom;
To embody your skillful means
Of adapting teaching according to capabilities;
To embody your fearless courage
To liberate all beings;
To embody the incisiveness
Of your unhindered eloquence.

Oh great, compassionate Buddha!
In order to propagate Buddhism:
Some of them leave their hometowns and travel to strange
　　　　lands far away;
Some of them lead the hard life of pioneers, cultivating the
　　　　land;
Some of them cross deserts all alone;
Some of them endure hunger and cold, and travel over
　　　　mountains and valleys.
Traveling to propagate the Dharma:
Some of them suffer deprivations
And the hardships of war;
Some of them die in desolate areas
As a result of having accidents;

願他們追隨佛陀您的腳步——
　都能擁有您悲智雙運的精神，
　都能擁有您觀機逗教的權巧，
　都能擁有您度眾無畏的勇氣，
　都能擁有您辯才無礙的魄力。

慈悲偉大的佛陀！
他們為了弘揚佛法，
　有的背井離鄉，遠渡重洋；
　有的篳路藍縷，披荊斬刺；
　有的孤身隻影，橫渡流沙；
　有的忍受饑寒，攀山越嶺。
他們在弘法旅途中，
　有的因烽火戰亂而顛沛流離，
　有的因遭遇不測而埋骨荒郊，

Some of them sacrifice their lives
To protect Buddhism and the Sangha;
Some of them die before the fulfillment of their aspirations
Because they fall ill from persistent overwork.
In order to propagate the Dharma,
They accept adversity philosophically,
And are quite content, even when facing setbacks;
In order to liberate all beings,
They disregard praise and criticism
Without any grudge or regret.
Like the well-respected Purana—
The chief preacher among the ten great disciples of
　　　Sakyamuni,
Who conquered the barbarous Indra through samadhi;
Like the esteemed Maudgalyayana—
Another one of the ten great disciples of Sakyamuni,
Noted for his supernatural powers, who died for Buddhism;
Like the celebrated monk Daoan[27] of the Eastern Jin
　　　Dynasty,
Who toiled to propagate the Dharma;
Like the noted abbot Baizhang of the Tang Dynasty,
Who established the monastic rules of purity.
There have been even more people of virtue who propagate
The Dharma to benefit all beings;
They have left glorious chapters in the history of Buddhism.

有的因護教衛僧而捨身捨命，
有的因積勞成疾而壯志未酬。
他們為了弘法，
　　逆來順受，甘之如飴；
他們為了度眾，
　　不計毀譽，無怨無悔。
像富樓那尊者的化導蠻凶；
像目犍連尊者的為教殉難；
像道安[27]大師的奔波弘法；
像百丈大師的禪門清規；
還有更多弘法利生的善知識們，
　　為佛教寫下輝煌的篇章。

Oh great, compassionate Buddha!
In this contemporary era,
Wrong teachings are confusing, widely dispersed, and
    disorderly;
Utilitarianism runs rampant;
Religious authority and superstition are spread far and wide,
    and overflow;
Discipline and ethics are destroyed.
We need people of virtue
To illuminate the dark corners with your Buddha light,
To wash away the karma of wrongdoing from all beings with
    your cleansing Dharma-water.

Oh great, compassionate Buddha!
We pray to you to bless and protect
Their safe and peaceful opportunities, and
Their resolute minds that seek enlightenment;
We pray that they will
Be free from physical and mental sickness, and
Be able to break past hindrances and difficult situations.
May your Truth reach all beings
In the three thousand chilocosmos;
May your great Dharma be promoted and developed
In all nations.

慈悲偉大的佛陀！
今天的時代裡，
　　異說雜亂紛紜，
　　功利主義囂張，
　　神權迷信氾濫，
　　綱紀倫理破壞，
需要善知識們——
用您的佛光照亮幽暗的角落，
用您的法水洗滌眾生的罪業。

慈悲偉大的佛陀！
　　祈求您庇佑他們安全的機遇，
　　祈求您庇佑他們堅固的道心，
　　祈求您庇佑他們免除身心疾病，
　　祈求您庇佑他們突破障礙難關。
願您的真理能普及三千世界，
願您的大法能弘揚萬億國土。

Oh great, compassionate Buddha,
Please accept our sincerest prayer!
Oh great, compassionate Buddha,
Please accept our sincerest prayer!

慈悲偉大的佛陀!
請求您接受我至誠的祈願,
慈悲偉大的佛陀!
請求您接受我至誠的祈願。

A Prayer for a Visitation to a Buddhist Family

Oh great, compassionate Buddha!
Today we are gathering at the home
Of Mr. and Mrs. ____ :
To praise your greatness,
To have a delightful and thorough talk about the vastness
 and boundlessness of Buddhism,
To share the joy of the Dharma together.

Oh Buddha! We pray to you to shelter and protect
The family of Mr. and Mrs. ____ :
May they be healthy physically;
May their careers be trouble-free;
May their family be peaceful and safe;
May they be happy and fortunate.

We pray for your blessing
To support the family of Mr. and Mrs. ____ :
May they be in harmony, and respect each other;
May they be solicitous and considerate of each other;
May they be appreciative, and help each other,
May they cultivate merits, and form good affinity.

家庭普照祈願文

慈悲偉大的佛陀！
 今日我們大家聚集在
　○○先生和○○女士夫婦的府上，
我們大家讚美佛陀您的偉大，
我們暢談佛法的浩瀚無邊，
我們現在共同分享佛法的喜悅。

願佛陀您的覆護，
○○先生和○○女士全家老小，
　讓他們身體健康，讓他們事業順利，
　讓他們全家平安，讓他們如意吉祥。

願佛陀您的加被，
加持○○先生和○○女士全家眷屬，
　讓他們相互和敬，讓他們關愛體貼，
　讓他們感恩互助，讓他們培福結緣。

Today we gaze upon your dignified face and pray
For your respect-inspiring virtues
To influence Mr. and Mrs. ____ :
May they embody loving-kindness, compassion, joy, and equanimity
To create a Buddhist family together;
May they embody respect and tolerance
To study and cultivate meditation, purification, merits, and wisdom together.

We also pray for your compassion
To bless us all, as it has Mr. and Mrs. ____ ,
And seek your compassion and sympathy for us:
On the way leading to Buddhahood,
May we all progress zealously and never retreat;
In the ocean of the Dharma,
May we all inspire the correct belief and never retreat.

Oh great, compassionate Buddha!
Furthermore, we would like to tell you that,
In contemporary society,
Many families have been sick:
The generation gap between young and old;
The discord between in-laws;

今日我們仰望您的聖像金容，
願佛陀您的威德感召，
讓○○先生和○○女士的家人，
擁有慈悲喜捨，共同建立佛化家庭；
擁有尊重包容，共同修學禪淨福慧。

也請求佛陀您慈悲加被我們大家，
讓我們大家與
○○先生和○○女士夫婦一樣，
獲得佛陀您慈悲垂憐。
我們要在佛道上，精進不懈，永不退轉；
我們要在法海中，啟發正信，永不退心。

慈悲偉大的佛陀！
　我更要向您訴說，
今日的社會，不少家庭已經生病了，
　長幼之間的代溝，婆媳之間的不和，

The indulgence in seeking pleasure of children;
The habitual nagging and clinging of the old.
Still more, the difficulties of financial situations and the exhaustion of a career
Make every member of the family anxious and uncertain what to do, and
Make all their relatives worry and feel concerned.

Oh Buddha! We pray for your blessing and protection:
May this family
Fulfill their wish to seek wealth and security;
May this family
Be wholly complete in seeking harmony among family and relatives;
May this family
Obtain comfort and happiness in life as they wish;
May this family
Be successful in seeking careers and the future.

Oh great, compassionate Buddha!
Please grant them faith and happiness,
Please strengthen their fortitude and determination;
May they all obtain your sweet, dew-like, cleansing Dharma-water
Under the shine of your Buddha light.

子女喜好遊樂享受，長輩習於嘮叨執著。
還有財務生活的結据，
還有事業艱難的困頓，
使家中的份子，都在徬徨憂心；
使他們的親友，都在掛念關懷。

祈求佛陀您的庇佑，
讓這家人，求財富平安都能如願；
讓這家人，求眷屬和諧都能圓滿；
讓這家人，求生活安樂都能獲得；
讓這家人，求事業前途都能順遂。

慈悲偉大的佛陀！
請您賜給他們信心與歡喜，
請您增加他們堅忍與毅力，
讓他們在您的佛光普照之下，
　　都能夠獲得您的甘露法水。

Oh great, compassionate Buddha,
Please accept our sincerest prayers!
Oh great, compassionate Buddha,
Please accept our sincerest prayers!

慈悲偉大的佛陀!
請求您接受我的祈願,
慈悲偉大的佛陀!
請求您接受我的祈願。

A Prayer for the People
Who Listen to the Dharma

Oh great, compassionate Buddha!
We would like to pray for people who listen to the Dharma.
Please help us to obtain the joy of the Dharma;
Please help us to be understanding and open minded.
We certainly will heed and follow your teachings;
From this day forward,
We will strive to practice the Dharma.

Oh Buddha!
Please grant us healthy bodies and minds;
Please grant us harmonious families;
Please grant us successful careers;
Please grant us happy lives.

Oh great, compassionate Buddha!
You have given us the sweet, dew-like, cleansing Dharma-
 water;
You have given us the bright light of Truth;
You have given us the firm foundation of faith;
You have given us the boat of emancipation;
You have given us the compass of direction;
You have given us the truth of liberation.

為聽經聞法者祈願文

慈悲偉大的佛陀！
我要為所有聽經聞法的人祈願，
　　請您幫助我們獲得禪悅法喜，
　　請您幫助我們獲得心開意解。
我們對佛陀的教示，必然依教奉行；
我們對佛陀的真理，從此努力實踐；

希望佛陀您能賜給我們——健康的身心，
希望佛陀您能賜給我們——和樂的家庭，
希望佛陀您能賜給我們——順利的事業，
希望佛陀您能賜給我們——幸福的人生。

慈悲偉大的佛陀！
　　您給了我們甘露的法水，
　　您給了我們真理的明燈，您給了我們信心的柺杖，
　　您給了我們解脫的舟船，您給了我們指引的羅盤，
　　您給了我們得救的真理。

Oh great, compassionate Buddha!
We pray that the masses who listen to your teachings
Can practice the doctrines and
Can respectfully carry them out.
Furthermore, we pray that everyone
Can share the Dharma and Dharma joy
With relatives and friends;
Can share the Dharma and Dharma joy
With colleagues.
May we all come together to purify our minds;
May we all come together to beautify our society.

Oh great, compassionate Buddha!
Today, in spite of advancements
In science and technology, and
An abundance of materials and resources,
Materialism still abounds;
Public morality has been tainted;
Vexations flourish;
Crimes have increased daily.
We have not been at ease;
We have not been at peace.

慈悲偉大的佛陀！
祈願所有聽經聞法的大眾，
　　都能實踐佛陀的法義，都能奉行佛陀的教誨；
更希望大家
都能把佛法帶給親戚朋友們同沾法喜，
都能把佛法帶給工作同仁們共享法樂。
　　讓我們一起來淨化人心，
　　讓我們一起來美化社會。

慈悲偉大的佛陀！
今天的時代，
雖然科技進步，物質豐富；
但是物欲橫流，人心污染，
　　煩惱熾盛，犯罪日增。
大家過得並不自在，
大家過得並不安穩。

Oh great Buddha!
Please guide us in understanding cause and effect, and karmic
   retribution clearly;
Please guide us in exalting loving-kindness, compassion, joy,
   and equanimity;
Please guide us in respectfully upholding the five precepts and
   the ten wholesome conducts;
Please guide us in carrying out the six paramitas.
We hope to transfer the merits of listening to
The Buddha's teachings to all beings in the Dharma realms;
May we all seek and realize supreme Enlightenment.

Furthermore, Buddha, with your great power
We pray for your blessing and protection:
May our country have
An efficient government and people who enjoy peace;
May our society be plentiful and populous
And in a state of peace and good welfare;
May our economy prosper,
And grow steadily;
May our people live and work in peace and contentment,
Have good fortune, and have all their wishes fulfilled.

祈求偉大的佛陀——
　　您能加持我們明白因緣果報，
　　您能加持我們發揚慈悲喜捨，
　　您能加持我們奉行五戒十善，
　　您能加持我們實踐六波羅蜜。
我們願將聽者聞者的功德，
　　回向給法界眾生，讓大家求證無上菩提。

更祈求佛陀您的大力庇佑，
讓我們的國家，政通人和，國泰民安；
讓我們的社會，風調雨順，富庶安康；
讓我們的經濟，繁榮進步，穩定成長；
讓我們的民眾，安居樂業，吉祥如意。

Oh great, compassionate Buddha,
Please accept our sincerest prayer!
Oh great, compassionate Buddha,
Please accept our sincerest prayer!

慈悲偉大的佛陀!
請求您接受我至誠的祈願,
慈悲偉大的佛陀!
請求您接受我至誠的祈願。

A Prayer for Parents of Monastics

Oh great, compassionate Buddha!
Today, in an extremely respectful state of mind,
I would like to pray and bless my parents.
If not for the diligence and kindness of my parents
To nourish my physical body,
How would I have been able to grow to become an adult?
If not for the protection and care of my parents, day and night,
To rear and guide me,
How would I have been able to be educated and reasonable?
Now, even though I give up what I treasure
And bid farewell to my family to enter the monastery,
I will never forget the mountain-high affection
And ocean-deep kindness of my parents.

Oh great, compassionate Buddha!
With your power,
Please comfort my parents' body and mind;
Please protect the good fortune and good intentions of my
　　　　　parents;
Please let my parents deeply believe in cause and effect;
Please let my parents initiate Bodhi mind.
May my siblings completely fulfill their duties as children,
Enabling our parents to be secure about resources.

出家眾為父母祈願文

慈悲偉大的佛陀！
　我今天要以萬分恭敬的心情，
　來為我的父母祈願祝福。
如果不是父母辛勤劬勞，長養我的色身性命，
　我那裡能長大成人？
如果不是父母日夜護念，給予我的撫育教導，
　我那裡能知書達理？
如今，我雖然割愛辭親，皈投佛門，
但父母如山高的情義，如海深的恩惠，
　我一刻也不敢忘懷。

慈悲偉大的佛陀！
　請加持我的父母身心康泰，
　請庇佑我的父母吉祥如意，
　請讓我的父母能深信因果，
　請讓我的父母能發菩提心。
希望我的兄弟姊妹，
　能善盡為人子女的責任，
　讓父母在物質上不虞匱乏。

Oh great, compassionate Buddha!
I would like to unburden myself:
In their busy lives, my parents deeply cling to emotional
　　　　　　attachment
And it is hard for them to give up worldly things.
In fact, they should let go of their concern for the family
And their anxiety for their children.
Because children can take care of themselves,
Parents do not have to work too hard
For their children's future.
They should adjust to circumstances and let go;
Then they will be at ease and feel free from anxiety.

I hope my parents know
That my Dharma siblings are like their own children;
If parents have compassion and make vows,
Then all people become their children.

Oh Buddha, please look:
Mahinda,[28]
The reputable founder of Buddhism in Ceylon, and
　　　　　　Sanghamitta[29] of Ceylon;
Master Kuiji,[30]
The well-known disciple of Xuanzang in the Tang Dynasty;

慈悲偉大的佛陀！
我要向您傾訴：
我的父母在忙碌的人生裡，
　　情執深重，世法難捨，
他們對家庭的顧念，他們對子女的牽掛，
　　其實都應該放下。
因為，兒孫自有兒孫福，
　　莫為兒孫作馬牛。
他們對生活要能隨緣放下，才能自在，才能寬心。

我希望父母知道，
　　我的師兄弟都如同他們的兒女；
只要他們擁有悲心願力，
　　所有人都可以成為他們的兒女。

您看！
錫蘭的摩哂陀[28]和僧伽密多[29]，
唐朝的窺基大師[30]，

Master Jizang,[31]
Who compiled the collection of Madhamika School in the
 Sui Dynasty;
Yitian,[32]
The well-known imperial preceptor of Korea;
All of them were offered to the Buddhist faith by their fathers,
And all later went down in history for their lofty virtues.

Oh great, compassionate Buddha!
Although I am not gifted or quick-witted and am unable to
 attain
Even a small fraction of what past sages have accomplished,
I am willing to take their spirit as a model,
To strive for cultivation, to work hard on attending to the
 way,
And to propagate Buddhism to benefit all sentient beings.

Oh great, compassionate Buddha!
I will not be idle;
I vow to progress zealously.
May this slight token of my regard complete my filial piety;
May my parents, life after life:
Avoid falling into lower realms;
Distance themselves from vexation;
Encounter a Buddha-time;
Hear sutras and the Dharma.

隋代的吉藏大師[31]，
韓國的義天國師[32]，
　都是父親將他們奉獻給佛門，
　後來都名垂青史，功德巍巍。

慈悲偉大的佛陀！
我雖然資質愚魯，
　無法及於前賢的萬分之一；
但我願效法他們的精神，
　努力修持，用功辦道；
　弘揚佛法，饒益有情。

慈悲偉大的佛陀！
我不會懈怠，我要發心精進，
願以此微忱能圓滿我的孝心，
更願我的父母能生生世世，
　不墮惡道，遠離煩惱；
　值遇佛世，聽經聞法；

May my parents, under you,
Form good affinity with Dharma friends.

Oh great, compassionate Buddha,
Please accept my sincerest prayer!
Oh great, compassionate Buddha,
Please accept my sincerest prayer!

讓他們都能在您的座下，
共結菩提道友的善緣。

慈悲偉大的佛陀！
請求您接受我至誠的祈願。
慈悲偉大的佛陀！
請求您接受我至誠的祈願。

To nourish the Dharma body;
May he/she delve thoroughly into the vast deep ocean of the Dharma
To derive the taste of the Dharma.
Although I am only an ordinary person, I do thoroughly understand
That the assembly of the Sangha
Is a great furnace for molding virtuous people and sages,
That the assembly of the Sangha
Is the place of Buddhism to help one achieve the Buddhahood.
Like Master Huike,[33] the successor of Bodhidharma, in the South and North Dynasties,
Who cut off his arm and stood in the snow in an appeal to be received as a disciple,
And ultimately obtained great teachings;
Like Chan Master Fayuan[34] of the Song Dynasty,
Who thought nothing of humiliation,
And ultimately became a great monastic;
Like Chan Master Beidu,[35] a fifth-century monk
Who was able to cross a river in a wooden cup;
Like Chan Master Yinyuan[36] of the Ming Dynasty,
Who preached the Dharma in Japan;
All of them were attracted not to fame and profit,
But to preaching the Dharma and benefiting all beings.

長養法身；
讓他能深入法海，
汲取法味。
我雖一介凡愚，
也深深知道：
僧團是陶鑄聖賢的大洪爐，
僧團是造就龍象的選佛場。
慧可大師[33]立雪斷臂，
　終獲大法；
法遠禪師[34]不辭屈辱，
　終成大器；
杯度禪師[35]渡海到青山；
隱元禪師[36]弘法於扶桑；
他們不慕榮利，
　只為弘法利生。

Oh great, compassionate Buddha!
I am not praying for my child to support me with delicious food
Or glorify my family standing;
I am only praying for him/her to take time-honored sages as models,
And propagate Buddhism and liberate sentient beings.
Oh Buddha! So many words in my heart cannot completely express
My worries and expectations as a parent;
And yet I would like to tell you that:
Today, since I consent to my child entering the monastery,
Hereafter, I will support his/her Dharma practice that leads to Buddhahood.

Oh great, compassionate Buddha!
Once again I pray to you to protect my child:
Please grant him/her the vigorous determination
To endure rigorous trials;
Please grant him/her brave and great confidence
To endure the loneliness of seeking the Dharma;
Please grant him/her the supernatural power of wisdom
To survive the hindrances of the mind;
Please grant him/her firm thought that seeks enlightenment
To withstand external adversity.

慈悲偉大的佛陀！
我不求孩子甘旨奉養，
　　光耀門楣；
只求他能效法古德，
　　興教度眾。
佛陀！千言萬語，
　　道不盡為人父母的牽掛與期望，
但我要告訴佛陀您，
今天，我既然應允他出家，
爾後，我會維護他的道業。

慈悲偉大的佛陀！
再一次地祈求您庇佑他，
賜給他剛健的毅力，
　　讓他能受得了嚴峻的考驗；
賜給他勇猛的信心，
　　讓他能耐得住求法的寂寞；
賜給他般若的神力，
　　讓他能熬得過內心的魔障；
賜給他堅固的道念，
　　讓他能經得起外來的打擊。

Oh great, compassionate Buddha,
Please accept my sincerest prayer!
Oh great, compassionate Buddha,
Please accept my sincerest prayer!

慈悲偉大的佛陀！
請求您接受我至誠的祈願，
慈悲偉大的佛陀！
請求您接受我至誠的祈願。

A Prayer for the Dharma Service

Oh great, compassionate Buddha!
I am a pious devotee.
I like very much to participate in the Dharma Service in the
    monastery.
Whether chanting a Buddha's name or meditating,
I always look forward to it profoundly,
The birthdays of all Buddhas and bodhisattvas, and
I celebrate all with joy;
At the opening ceremony of a monastery
I am always excited;
In the Repentance Service of Emperor Liang,
Or the Repentance Service of Compassionate Samadhi Water,
I often participate whenever I can;
The Great Compassion Repentance Ceremony,
Stirs me even more;
At the offering of light or pilgrimage,
I am also happy to join others in these worthy activities.

Oh Buddha!
I would like to report to you:
Whenever I participate in the Dharma Service
Is the best time for communication with you;
Whenever I interact with others at Dharma Services,

共修法會祈願文

慈悲偉大的佛陀！
　我是一個虔誠的在家信徒，
　我很喜歡參加寺院的共修法會，
念佛、禪坐，
　我總是深心嚮往；
諸佛菩薩的聖誕，
　我都歡喜慶祝；
寺院的開光落成，
　我都非常興奮；
梁皇、水懺，我時常隨喜參加；
大悲懺法會，
　我更是十分喜愛。
獻燈、朝山，我也樂於共襄盛舉。

我要向佛陀您報告：
　每次參加共修法會，
　是我最好和您交流的時候；
　每次利用共修活動，

I always receive your pure and cool Dharma water with respect.

During the Dharma Service,
I attain the joy of the Dharma;
I feel my mind opened and liberated intellectually.
Seeing the Dharma brothers and sisters in the Dharma Service,
Right away I raise Dharma affinities and Dharma affection;
Right away I feel the harmony of the dharma realms.
Steeped in the auspicious and peaceful atmosphere,
All the gossip of people is instantly behind me;
Ignorance and worries immediately disappear, without a trace.
How I enjoy these Dharma Services!
For they are meetings in taking the Dharma as fellowship,
They are taking the Dharma as teachers,
They are taking the Dharma as the path,
They are taking the Dharma as joy.
In our Dharma Service
There are people of virtue and the elderly
To open up the treasury of truth and indicate its meaning,
There is good company of the same belief to assist us.
I feel profoundly grateful for these complete, good conditions,
I profoundly cherish being human.

Oh great, compassionate Buddha!
I am willing to follow your teachings and admonitions,

我都仰承您的清涼法水。

在共修法會裡，
　　我得到禪悅法喜，我覺得心開意解。
看到共修的師兄師姊們，
我就昇起道情法愛，我就感到法界和諧；
沐浴在共修的祥和氣氛裡，
　　人我是非，頓時拋在腦後；
　　無明煩惱，立刻消失無形。
我是多麼喜歡法會啊！因為——
　　法會，是以法為會，法會，是以法為師，
　　法會，是以法為軌，法會，是以法為樂。
我們在共修法會中，
有大德長者的開示，
有善友同修的提攜，
　　我深深感恩善緣具足，
　　我深深珍惜人身難得。

慈悲偉大的佛陀！
　　我願遵循您的教誨，

I am willing to follow your doctrines;
I will exalt your spirit of joyous giving to benefit others
And serve society;
I will follow your model of propagating the Dharma and
        benefiting all beings,
And progress zealously without ceasing.

Oh Buddha! Great Buddha!
I attend the Dharma Service again and again;
I pray to you again and again:
That you support us with compassion;
That you guide us with wisdom;
That you bless and protect us with brightness;
That you refresh us with sweet dew.
May our bodies be in good health;
May our careers be carefree, without obstruction;
May our families be blissful and happy;
May our minds be pure, auspicious, and peaceful;
May our society be harmonious and joyous;
May our country be prosperous, peaceful, and safe;
May we all be respectful and tolerant of each other,
May we all be wholly satisfied and at ease.

我願奉行您的法義，
我要發揚您喜捨利他的精神，服務社會；
我要追隨您弘法利生的腳步，精進不懈。

佛陀！偉大的佛陀！
我一次又一次地參加共修，
我一次又一次地向您祈求，
祈求您以慈悲加持我們，祈求您以智慧引導我們，
祈求您以光明庇佑我們，祈求您以甘露滋潤我們，
讓我們的身體能夠健康無恙，
讓我們的事業能夠通達順暢，
讓我們的家庭能夠幸福美滿，
讓我們的心靈能夠淨化祥和，
讓我們的社會能夠融和歡喜，
讓我們的國家能夠繁榮安康，
讓我們都能尊重包容，
讓我們都能圓滿自在。

Oh great, compassionate Buddha,
Please accept my sincerest prayers!
Oh great, compassionate Buddha,
Please accept my sincerest prayers!

慈悲偉大的佛陀！
請求您接受我至誠的祈願，
慈悲偉大的佛陀！
請求您接受我至誠的祈願。

A Prayer to Amitabha Buddha

Oh great, compassionate Amitabha Buddha!
In an extremely respectful and sincere state of mind,
Every day I come before you
To chant your name and to pay respect to your golden image;
The ray of light sent from your white curling hair illuminates
　　　the whole universe,
Your Dharma-eye is as crystal-clear as the ocean.
We extend our heartfelt thanks to you
For initiating the forty-eight vows to liberate us
Many periods of time ago,
And for adorning the Pure Land of the Ultimate Bliss
By wholly completing the way leading to Buddhahood
More than ten kalpas ago.

Where you are,
There are clusters of lotus flowers in the seven-jewel pond,
Soft, pure, and cool water of the eight virtues,
Orderly lined trees and towers,
Frequent mind-soothing and mind-pleasing fragrant breezes,
Dharma-voice and wonderful music floating everywhere,
Exotic flowers and unusual birds preaching the Dharma,
Sufficient clothing and food appearing as one's heart wishes,
All excellent beings gathering in one place,
And offerings to all Buddhas every daybreak.

向阿彌陀佛祈願文

慈悲偉大的阿彌陀佛！
　我每天來到您的座前，
　以極為恭敬虔誠的心情，
　稱念您的聖號，禮拜您的金容，
您的白毫光明照亮整個宇宙，
您的法眼有如海水一樣清澈。
我們由衷地感謝您在久遠劫前，
　發四十八願救度我們。
您於十劫前圓滿佛道，
　莊嚴了極樂淨土。

您那裡，
　七寶池中蓮華朵朵，八功德水柔軟清涼，
　行樹樓閣井然有序，香風時來舒悅眾心，
　梵音妙樂處處飄盪，奇花異鳥宣揚佛法，
　衣食無缺隨心所現，諸上善人聚會一處，
　每日清旦供養諸佛。

Where you are,
Pure Land of the Ultimate Bliss—There is no environmental pollution;
Economics—There is no confiscation of property;
Life—There is no cruelty;
Dealing with people—There is no gossip;
Circle of friends—There is no misunderstanding;
Politics—There is no persecution;
Transportation—There are no troublesome incidents;
Society—There is no distinction in class.

Oh great, compassionate Amitabha Buddha!
I would like to unburden myself to you:
In our impure world,
There is deception and fraud among people,
There are unceasing conflicts among countries.
Our suffering is as deep as the ocean,
Our worries spread like creeping weeds.

Oh great, compassionate Amitabha Buddha!
I pray to you to receive me through your compassionate vows.
In my sleep:
May I see your golden body;
May I travel to and experience your Pure Land;

您那裡，
　國土，沒有環境的污染；
　經濟，沒有財產的佔有；
　生活，沒有惡人的殘害；
　處眾，沒有人我的是非；
　交遊，沒有猜疑的誤會；
　政治，沒有迫害的冤屈；
　交通，沒有事故的發生；
　社會，沒有階級的差別。

慈悲偉大的阿彌陀佛！
我要向您傾訴，
在我們這個五濁惡世裡，
　人與人之間爾虞我詐，國與國之間紛爭不息，
我們的憂苦如大海般的深沉，
我們的煩惱像蔓草般的綿延。

慈悲偉大的阿彌陀佛！
祈求您以慈誓攝受我，
願我在夢寐之際，
　能夠見到您的金身，能夠遊歷您的淨土，

May I obtain your blessing by the sprinkling of your Dharma-
    water;
May I obtain the touch and illumination of your light;
May I eliminate past karma;
May I increase good roots;
May I decrease afflictions;
May I enhance the effectiveness of my vow.

I pray to you to liberate and convince me
With your compassionate heart;
When my time in the world has ended,
May I know it beforehand,
And not suffer from physical illness;
May I have no mental delusions
And have clear, correct views.

I pray to you, all Buddhas and bodhisattvas,
To hold the light-emitting golden tower in your hands
To receive and guide all beings;
May all experienced and knowledgeable people
Be joyous and appreciative,
Initiate the bodhi mind, hear the wonderful sound of the
    Dharma,
And possess "the patience of non-arising of life and dharma";

能夠得到您的甘露灌頂，能夠得到您的光明觸照，
讓我消除宿業，讓我增長善根，
讓我減少煩惱，讓我提昇願力。

祈求您以悲心度化我，
讓我在世緣已了時，
　　能夠預知時至，身無病苦；
　　能夠心無顛倒，正念分明。

祈求您和菩薩聖眾，
　　手持金台，放光接引；
讓所有見聞的人，
　　都能歡喜讚歎，發菩提心；
　　都能聞妙法音，獲無生忍；
讓我能夠得到您的授記，
　　乘願再來，弘法利生；

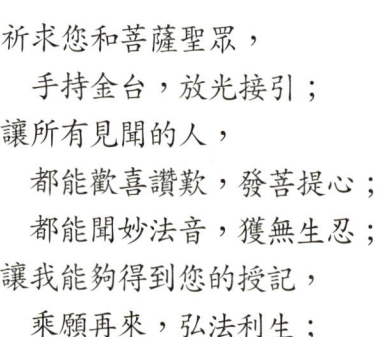

May I obtain your blessings,
And come back again with vows to propagate the Dharma
    and benefit all beings;
May all sentient beings be reborn in the Pure Land of the
    West,
And never regress.

Oh great, compassionate Amitabha Buddha,
Please accept my sincerest prayer!
Oh great, compassionate Amitabha Buddha,
Please accept my sincerest prayer!

願所有的眾生,
都能夠同生西方,
永不退轉。

慈悲偉大的佛陀!
請求您接受我至誠的祈願,
慈悲偉大的佛陀!
請求您接受我至誠的祈願。

A Prayer to the Medicine Buddha

Oh great, compassionate Medicine Buddha!
Please listen to my report.
There is truly too much suffering in the world these days:
The crimes of arson, murder, and theft;
The cruel oppression of corrupt officials;
The turbulence of politics and the economy;
The disasters of earth, water, fire, and wind;
All these often make people lose everything they own
In the blink of an eye.
The suffering of being bedridden with a lingering illness
Resulting from an imbalance of the four great elements;
Even heroes moan and groan and have difficulty being at ease;
The sea of karma that is full of passions and delusions
Resulting from greed, anger, and ignorance
Rolls unceasingly like roaring waves and billows.

Oh great, compassionate Medicine Buddha!
If we do not depend on you now,
How can we escape the sea of suffering?
If we do not rely on you now,
How can we subdue our defilements and resentments?
Today, I sincerely chant your name, and

向藥師如來祈願文

慈悲偉大的藥師如來!
　請您垂聽我的報告,
今天世界上的苦難實在是太多了!
　燒殺擄掠的侵犯,貪官污吏的迫害,
　政治經濟的動盪,地水火風的災變,
往往使人們在瞬息之間,
　失去了所有的一切。
那四大不調,纏綿病榻的痛苦,
　即使英雄好漢也呻吟難安;
那貪瞋愚癡,煩惱叢生的業海,
　有如波濤洶湧地翻滾不停。

慈悲偉大的藥師如來!
　我們再不倚靠您,如何出離苦海?
　我們再不仰仗您,如何降伏怨魔?
我今天虔誠地——

Pay respect to your image,
Not to ask you only to bless myself,
But to hope that all beings obtain your great protection
To live and work in peace and contentment,
And in happiness and harmony.

Oh great, compassionate Medicine Buddha!
We understand thoroughly:
That, in this world of impurity,
All natural disasters and man-made calamities
Are caused by collective karma;
That, on this impure, mundane earth,
Physical and mental suffering
Is caused by the passions and delusions of life.
If we want to thoroughly eliminate calamities and disasters,
We must first eliminate the karma of our own wrongdoings;
If we want to establish the Pure Land of the East,
We must first purify our bodies and minds.
Therefore, I would like to pray to you, Medicine Buddha,
To eliminate our greed and anger,
To eliminate our ignorance and struggles.
We are willing to transfer all our good-rooted merits
To all beings in the dharma realms.
May everyone live freely
And everything turn out as they wish.

稱念您的名號，禮敬您的聖容，
不只是祈求您能加被我個人，
更希望眾生都得到您的庇護，
安居樂業，歡喜融和。

慈悲偉大的藥師如來！
我們深知在這個五濁惡世裡，
　天災人禍是共業所感召；
在這個娑婆穢土中，
　身心疾苦是煩惱所造成。
如果要徹底消除災難，
　先得消除自己的罪業；
如果要建立琉璃淨土，
　先得淨化自己的身心。
所以我要祈求藥師如來您，
　消除我們的貪婪瞋恚，
　消除我們的無明鬥爭。
我們願將所有善根功德，
　回向法界一切眾生。
讓大家都能 —— 生活自在，事事如意。

Furthermore, great, compassionate Medicine Buddha!
I pray to you to bestow your great power on us for protection;
I will undertake the following, pure, original vows:
First vow: May all sentient beings be equal and at ease;
Second vow: May all undertakings benefit the masses;
Third vow: May panic and terror be kept far away;
Fourth vow: May all sentient beings calmly uphold bodhi;
Fifth vow: May man-made calamities and natural disasters disappear completely;
Sixth vow: May all physically-challenged beings be rehabilitated back to normal;
Seventh vow: May all beings suffering from diseases be restored to health;
Eighth vow: May all human relations foster mutual understanding and harmony;
Ninth vow: May all beings with wrong views turn over a new leaf;
Tenth vow: May all prisoners suffering unjustly come to know justice;
Eleventh vow: May society and the masses live in affluence;
Twelfth vow: May all beings be tolerant and respectful.

慈悲偉大的藥師如來！
更祈求您以神力加被我們，
我在您的面前也發如是清淨本願：
　第一願：願所有眾生平等自在，
　第二願：願所作事業利益大眾，
　第三願：願驚慌恐怖從此遠離，
　第四願：願一切有情安住菩提，
　第五願：願天災人禍消失無形，
　第六願：願殘缺眾生復健正常，
　第七願：願病苦眾生恢復健康，
　第八願：願人際關係溝通調和，
　第九願：願邪見眾生改邪歸正，
　第十願：願受冤囚者平反冤屈，
　第十一願：願社會大眾豐衣足食，
　第十二願：願所有眾生包容尊重。

Oh great, compassionate Medicine Buddha!
We make offerings to you
With our pure deeds of body, mouth, and mind;
We take you as our model
With our zealous progress in the study of precept, meditation,
    and wisdom;
I pray that you give, with your great compassion,
Your respect-inspiring virtues all over the dharma realms
To fulfill our wishes,
To let our human world also establish the Pure Land of the
    East.

Oh great, compassionate Medicine Buddha,
Please accept my sincerest prayer!
Oh great, compassionate Medicine Buddha,
Please accept my sincerest prayer!

慈悲偉大的藥師如來！
　我們以清淨的身口意業供養您，
　我們以精進的戒定慧學效法您，
祈求您施捨大慈大悲，
　將您的威德遍滿法界，
　滿足我們的願望，
　讓我們人間也能建設琉璃淨土。

慈悲偉大的藥師如來！
請求您接受我至誠的祈願！
慈悲偉大的藥師如來！
請求您接受我至誠的祈願！

A Prayer to Avalokitesvara Bodhisattva

Oh great, compassionate Avalokitesvara Bodhisattva!
Please relieve the distressed and the suffering.
Please listen compassionately
To your disciple confess and repent:
Since I have come to know human affairs,
I always feel that life is not peaceful;
I often feel that circumstances are not agreeable.
Towards relatives and good friends,
I am not considerate or helpful enough;
Towards society and the masses,
I lack skillful means to bring harmony to all people.

Oh great, compassionate Avalokitesvara Bodhisattva!
Whenever I look up at your compassionate image,
My mind indeed feels pure and at ease;
Whenever I chant your name,
My spirit indeed feels comfortable, and I myself feel free
　　　　from worldly worries.
Facing you, who are dignified and immaculate,
I feel so ashamed!
In comparison to your sprinkling sweet dew all over
To universally benefit humans and devas:
You are like an ocean, I am like well water;

向觀世音菩薩祈願文

慈悲偉大的觀世音菩薩！
　請您救苦救難，
　慈悲地垂聽弟子的發露懺悔：
我自懂事以來，總覺得生命不很安穩；
我在世間生活，常感到事情不很適意；
我對親朋好友，缺乏照顧幫忙；
我對社會大眾，不能周遍圓融。

慈悲偉大的觀世音菩薩！
每當我仰望您的慈容時，
　我的心靈才感到清涼自在；
每當我稱念您的聖號時，
　我的精神才得到解脫舒暢。
面對聖潔的您，我感到好慚愧啊！
和您的遍灑甘露，
普利人天比起來，
　您如海洋，我似井水；

You are like the sun and the moon, I am like a firefly;
You are like mountains, I am like a mole hill;
You are like a lion king, I am like a small mouse.

Oh great, compassionate Avalokitesvara Bodhisattva!
Over many kalpas, you have worked diligently in defiance of hardships,
And still want to return to the world to liberate all sentient beings.
You have done what is difficult for people to do
And still want to follow the world's cries to relieve its suffering.
Who am I?
Why can I not do the same?

Oh great, compassionate Avalokitesvara Bodhisattva!
I pray to you to guide me with your universal vows,
I pray to you to enlighten me with your compassionate vows.
May I have your fearless penetration
Of the nature of all things through wisdom:
If I face people of vices they will be transformed;
If I face villians their anger will be cooled;
If I face evil, the evil mind will be brought under control;
If I face the ignorant, they will obtain great wisdom.

您如日月,我似螢光;
您如山岳,我似丘陵;
您如獅王,我似小鼠。
慈悲偉大的觀世音菩薩!
您累劫勤苦,還要倒駕慈航;
您難行能行,還要尋聲救苦。
我何人也?
我何不能!

慈悲偉大的觀世音菩薩!
祈求您以弘誓攝我,祈求您以悲願度我。
讓我能擁有您的無畏圓通,
我若向惡人,惡人自感化;
我若向暴徒,瞋怒自息滅;
我若向魔外,邪心自調伏;
我若向愚癡,當得大智慧。

Oh great, compassionate Avalokitesvara Bodhisattva!
I pray to you to shelter me in your compassionate cloud;
I would like to learn your spirit of benefiting and relieving all beings:
To observe the needs of all beings through compassionate eyes;
To listen to the suffering of all beings with attentive ears;
To comfort the vexations and anxiety of all beings with wonderful words;
To soothe the wounds of all beings with both hands.

Oh great, compassionate Avalokitesvara Bodhisattva!
I pray to you to illuminate us with your light of wisdom:
I will assist all beings through joyous giving;
I will convert and guide the stubborn into the Truth by cooperating with and adapting to them;
I will provide people with convenience through beneficial conduct;
I will help people to be happy through loving words.

Oh great, compassionate Avalokitesvara Bodhisattva!
I would like to take your liberation and ease as a model. From now on:
I will distance myself from contrary and delusive ideas
To contemplate the ease of the individual;
I will distance myself from discrimination and personal conjecture

慈悲偉大的觀世音菩薩！
祈求您以慈雲覆我，
我要學習您利濟群生的精神，
　　用慈眼觀察眾生的需求，
　　用耳朵傾聽眾生的痛苦，
　　用美言安慰眾生的煩憂，
　　用雙手撫平眾生的創傷。

慈悲偉大的觀世音菩薩！
祈求您以智光照我，
　　我要用喜捨攝取眾生，
　　我要用同事化導頑強，
　　我要用利行給人方便，
　　我要用愛語助人歡喜。

慈悲偉大的觀世音菩薩！
我要以您的解脫自在為榜樣，
從今以後，
　　我要遠離顛倒妄想，觀人自在；
　　我要遠離分別臆測，觀境自在；

To contemplate the ease of circumstances;
I will distance myself from attachment and entanglement
To contemplate the ease of affairs;
I will distance myself from the five desires and the trouble of
      the world
To contemplate the ease of the mind.

Oh great, compassionate Avalokitesvara Bodhisattva,
Please accept my sincerest prayer!
Oh great, compassionate Avalokitesvara Bodhisattva,
Please accept my sincerest prayer!

我要遠離執著纏縛，觀事自在；
我要遠離五欲塵勞，觀心自在。

慈悲偉大的觀世音菩薩！
請求您接受我至誠的祈願，
慈悲偉大的觀世音菩薩！
請求您接受我至誠的祈願。

A Prayer for Devoir Chanting in Three Periods

Oh great, compassionate Amitabha Buddha!
Today, we come before you
To attend the Ceremony of Devoir Chanting in Three Periods for _____ .
In a respectful state of mind, we exalt your Pure Land;
With a pious voice, we praise the radiance of your sacred virtues.
In the Pure Land of the Ultimate Bliss that you have accomplished:
The palace and treasures are majestic,
The garden is clean and pure, and fruits and flowers flourish,
The Dharma-voice and wonderful music are everywhere,
All excellent beings are gathered in one place.
As for the wonderful and profound golden body that you manifest:
The ray of light that is sent
From the curl between your eyebrows brightens all worlds;
It touches and illuminates all beings so that they are all liberated;
The clearness of your Buddha eyes
Is as deep and broad as the ocean;
It treats all beings of Buddha Nature equally.

為三時繫念祈願文

慈悲偉大的阿彌陀佛！
我們今天來到您的座前，
參加〇〇君的三時繫念法會，
我們以恭敬的心意，
　讚頌您的佛國淨土；
我們以虔誠的音聲，
　歌詠您的聖德光輝。
您所成就的極樂世界——
　宮殿城闕百寶莊嚴，
　園林清淨華果茂盛，
　梵音妙樂周遍國界，
　諸上善人聚會一處。
您所具有的妙好金身——
　眉間白毫光明萬丈，
　觸照眾生悉皆得度；
　紺目澄清深廣如海，
　等視一切悉如佛子。

Oh great, compassionate Amitabha Buddha!
The life of ____ , a devout Buddhist, has ended;
His/her mind is tired and is no longer willing
To ride in this worn-out vehicle to travel the world;
He/she only hopes to find a safe place,
As an everlasting support.
At this very moment, we can only pray to you
To guide him/her to the Pure Land of the West:
May the lotus pond of the seven-jewels nourish his/her wisdom life;
May the water of the eight virtues cleanse his/her vexation;
May the avenues of jewel-trees and Indra's net of gems brush away his/her worldly worries;
May the preaching of the Dharma of waterbirds treat his/her wounds.

I also would like to exhort _____ :
Please abandon attachment to the body and mind;
Please let go of the entanglement of affection and hatred;
Please forget the grief and suffering of the past;
Please put the distractions of the world behind;
Please use your wholehearted, sincere repentance
To welcome Amitabha Buddha;
Please pray to Amitabha Buddha
With the chanting of clear, continuous thought after thought;

慈悲偉大的阿彌陀佛！
○○居士一期的生命已盡，
他疲倦的心識，
　　不願再乘著破車行走娑婆，
只希望找尋一處安全的地方，
　　作為永久的依靠。
此時此刻，唯有祈求您，
引導他來到您的佛國淨土，
　　讓七寶蓮池長養他的慧命，
　　讓八功德水滌淨他的煩憂，
　　讓行樹寶網拂去他的塵勞，
　　讓水鳥說法療治他的創傷。

我也要勸請○○居士，
　　請你捨棄身心的執著，
　　請你放下愛恨的糾纏，
　　請你忘卻過去的憂苦，
　　請你拋開塵世的雜念；
用一心虔誠的懺悔，迎接阿彌陀佛；
用念念分明的佛號，祈求阿彌陀佛；

Please make offerings to Amitabha Buddha
With a clear and pure mind;
Please follow Amitabha Buddha
With joyful steps.
From now on, may you rest in the Buddha's land and be free of rebirth;
From now on, may your pure thoughts continue and may you complete the perfect state of Buddhahood.
When we see each other in the future,
May you already be enlightened and in nirvana;
When we meet each other in the future,
May you already have acted on your vow to come back again to liberate sentient beings.

Oh great, compassionate Amitabha Buddha!
We would like to show our gratitude to you
For your teachings and admonitions;
We would like to remember the teaching of Venerable Zhongfeng,[37]
An Imperial preceptor in the Song Dynasty, with gratitude.
May we know that absence of suffering is utmost joy;
May we understand that our own Buddha Nature is our own home;
May we understand that cutting off the attachments associated with the six sense organs

用清清淨淨的心意，供養阿彌陀佛；
用歡歡喜喜的腳步，追隨阿彌陀佛。
從此，
　　安住佛國，遠離輪迴；
從此，
　　淨念相續，圓成佛果。
希望來日再見時，
　　你已花開見佛悟無生；
希望他日相逢時，
　　你已乘願再來度有情。

慈悲偉大的阿彌陀佛！
我們要感恩您的教誨，
我們要感念中峰國師[37]的開示，
　　讓我們知道「眾苦不侵稱極樂」，
　　讓我們明白「自性彌陀是吾家」，
　　讓我們懂得「六根坐斷蓮台現」，

Will bring enlightenment;
May we realize that the Pure Land of the West
Appears where our mind is.
We pray to transfer the merit of this Buddhist Service
To all beings in the dharma realms:
May the deceased reach the Pure Land
And achieve the supreme, perfect bodhi;
May the living diligently cultivate the three studies
And attain enlightenment together.

Oh great, compassionate Amitabha Buddha,
Please accept my sincerest prayer!
Oh great, compassionate Amitabha Buddha,
Please accept my sincerest prayer!

讓我們體悟「西方淨土隨心生」。
祈願以此佛事功德，
　　回向給法界一切眾生，
　　讓亡者速登極樂，早成佛道；
　　讓生者勤修三學，共證菩提。

慈悲偉大的阿彌陀佛！
請求您接受我至誠的祈願，
慈悲偉大的阿彌陀佛！
請求您接受我至誠的祈願。

A Prayer for the Repentance Service of Emperor Liang

Oh great, compassionate Buddha!
Through innumerable kalpas,
We, ordinary beings,
Have created infinite unwholesome karma;
Thank you, Buddha,
For granting us the method for repenting
To wash away and cleanse our impure bodies and minds,
To let us escape the prison of worries and suffering,
And start anew.

Like Ajatasatru,[38] a king of Magadha
Who killed his father, King Bimbisara, and later repented,
And was able to eliminate such evil karma;
Like Empress Chi of the Liang Dynasty,
Who repented
And was able to avert suffering and obtain happiness;
Like Yuan Liaofan[39] of the Ming Dynasty,
Who repented
And was able to obtain what he wished for;
Like Sun Qingyang,
Whose countenance became more elegant
Because of paying reverence.

梁皇寶懺祈願文

慈悲偉大的佛陀！
　無始劫來，
　我們凡愚眾生
　不知道造下了多少惡業，
感謝佛陀您賜給我們懺悔的方法，
洗滌我們污穢的身心，
讓我們得以躍出憂苦的牢籠，重新出發。

像阿闍世[38]因悔罪而消除惡業，
像郗氏皇后因懺悔而離苦得樂，
像袁了凡[39]因悔改而所求如願，
像孫清揚因禮拜而顏面圓滿。

They left anecdotes of repentance for the world to eliminate wrongdoings
And also established models of the courage to correct mistakes.

Oh great, compassionate Buddha!
"All the unwholesome karma that was created in the past
"By greed, anger, and ignorance
"In innumerable kalpas,
"And from the body, speech, and mind:
"I now repent them all."
In the life of this human world,
We often become slaves to love and affection,
Because our eyes indulge in all physical forms;
We often misunderstand our purity of intrinsic nature,
Because our ears grasp at sounds;
We often accept the mundane conditions of the world,
Because our noses cling to fragrance;
We often commit the boundless karma of wrongdoings,
Because our mouths speak harsh words;
We often encroach on others' possessions,
Because our bodies desire worldly matters;
We often accumulate many worries,
Because our minds arouse greed, anger, and ignorance.

他們為世間留下懺悔滅罪的佳話，
　也為後人留下勇於改過的典範。

慈悲偉大的佛陀！
「往昔所造諸惡業，皆由無始貪瞋癡，
　　從身語意之所生，一切我今皆懺悔。」
我們在人間的生活——
往往因眼根貪著諸色，
　作了恩愛的奴隸；
往往因耳根追逐音聲，
　迷惑本性的清淨；
往往因鼻根執著香氣，
　染著世間的塵緣；
往往因舌根口出惡言，
　犯下無邊的罪業；
往往因身根貪戀世間，
　侵害別人的所有；
往往因意根起貪瞋癡，
　積聚許多的煩惱。

All these vices are truly deep, vast, and boundless;
Until now, recalling these, I have cried bitterly,
And am extremely ashamed and regretful;
I can only follow the model
Of the Repentance Service of Emperor Liang
To prostrate myself sincerely and openly state
My past karma of wrongdoings:
Please bless me with your great light;
Please protect and support me with your compassion:
To reinforce my strength;
To fortify my benevolent thoughts;
To allow my past wrongdoings to be quickly eliminated;
To allow my future wrongdoings to be averted.
From this day on:
I will learn to observe with eyes of compassion,
Eyes of wisdom, eyes of Dharma, and eyes of Buddha,
To clearly understand the true reality of the world;
I will learn to be a good listener, to listen attentively,
To listen to both sides, and to listen thoroughly, to
   prevent gossip;
I will learn to speak kind words, to do good deeds,
And to have good intentions to spread the seeds of "the
   Three Goods";

種種罪惡，可謂深廣無邊，
至今想來，涕淚交流，愧悔無比，
只有依照梁皇寶懺的儀軌，
　虔誠頂禮，披陳往昔的罪業，
祈求您放光加被，
祈求您慈悲護持，
　增上我的力量，堅定我的善念，
　讓我已作之罪，迅速滅除；
　讓我未作之罪，不再復造。
自今爾後，
我要學習以慈眼慧眼法眼佛眼，
　洞察世間的實相；
我要學習用善聽諦聽兼聽全聽，
　免除人我的是非；
我要學習說愛語、做善事、存好心，
　散播「三好」的種子；

I will learn to have regard for kindness and justice,
       morality and gratitude,
To promote the moral principles of "the Three
       Righteousnesses."

Oh great, compassionate Buddha!
Please give witness:
May all the merits of all good roots of repentance
Be transferred to Anuttara-samyak-sambodhi,
The unexcelled complete enlightenment.
May all sentient beings in the dharma realms:
Eliminate the hindrance of past karma,
And have all their senses be free from defilement;
Have no anxiety and have no anger,
And be happy and peaceful;
Be free from fear and be at ease without obstacles;
Be reborn in the Pure Land together and attain nirvana.

Oh great, compassionate Buddha,
Please accept my sincerest prayer!
Oh great, compassionate Buddha,
Please accept my sincerest prayer!

我要學習講仁義、講道義、講恩義，
　　發揚「三義」的氣節。

慈悲偉大的佛陀！
請求您俯垂鑑證，
　　祈願所有懺悔善根，
　　悉皆回向阿耨多羅三藐三菩提。
願法界一切眾生——
　　業障消除，諸根清淨；
　　無諸憂惱，快意安然；
　　遠離畏懼，自在無礙；
　　共生淨土，同登彼岸。

慈悲偉大的佛陀！
請求您接受我至誠的祈願。
慈悲偉大的佛陀！
請求您接受我至誠的祈願。

A Prayer for the Repentance Service of Compassionate Samadhi Water

Oh great, compassionate Buddha!
Today, in a cautious and apprehensive state of mind,
Your disciples kneel before you
To participate in the Repentance Service of
 Compassionate Samadhi Water,
To confess and repent the karma from our past
 wrongdoings.

Oh great, compassionate Buddha!
Since transmigration that has existed without beginning,
I may have disrespected the Triple Gem,
And not been devoted to my parents;
I may have committed killing, stealing, sexual
 misconduct, and lying,
And disturbed all beings;
I may have been greedy, and vexed,
And indulged in the pleasures of easy lives;
I may have exalted myself and depreciated others,
And slandered virtuous ones and sages;
I may have doubted the relation between cause and effect
And had wrong views, ignorance, and delusion.

慈悲三昧水懺祈願文

慈悲偉大的佛陀！
　弟子等今天匍匐在您的座前，
　依照慈悲三昧水懺法，
　以戒慎惶恐的心情，
　向您發露懺悔往昔的罪業。

慈悲偉大的佛陀！
無始以來，我或許曾經──
　輕慢三寶，不孝父母，
　殺盜淫妄，擾亂眾生，
　貪欲煩惱，耽著逸樂，
　貢高我慢，毀謗聖賢，
　謗無因果，邪見愚癡。

Now, we are all here to pray for your compassion and to repent.
We pray for your sympathy and acceptance:
May our inner, ignorant delusions
Be illuminated by the bright lamp of repentance;
May the flame of our afflictions
Be extinguished by the sweet dew of repentance;
May the powerful current of our greed
Be obstructed by the dikes and dams of repentance;
May the high mountain of our arrogance
Be leveled by the giant shovel of repentance;
May the weapons of jealousy and hatred
Be destroyed by the power of repentance;
May the wound of our fear
Be eased by the comfort of repentance;
May the chronic disease of our indulgence
Be cured by the medicine of repentance;
May the muddy waters of ill will
Be purified by the pure drop of repentance.

Oh great, compassionate Buddha!
From now on, I will beautify life with compassion;
From now on, I will purify society with joyous giving;
From now on, I will bear responsibility with both shoulders;
From now on, I will tolerate everything with respect.

如今，弟子等在此求哀懺悔，
祈求慈悲偉大的佛陀哀愍納受，
願我們內心的癡暗，能因懺悔的明燈而照亮；
願我們煩惱的火焰，能因懺悔的甘霖而熄滅；
願我們貪慾的洪流，能因懺悔的堤壩而阻斷；
願我們憍慢的高山，能因懺悔的巨鏟而推平；
願我們嫉恨的刀箭，能因懺悔的力量而損毀；
願我們恐懼的創傷，能因懺悔的慰藉而安穩；
願我們放逸的沉痾，能因懺悔的藥草而治癒；
願我們怨懟的濁水，能因懺悔的清珠而潔淨。

慈悲偉大的佛陀！
今後，我要用慈悲來美化人生，
今後，我要用喜捨來淨化社會，
今後，我要用雙肩來承擔責任，
今後，我要用尊重來包容一切。

Please bless us with the Buddha light:
May we no longer adhere to unwholesome karma;
May we no longer create new wrongdoings;
May we no longer disregard cause and effect;
May we no longer forget and lose faith.
Please protect us with compassionate clouds:
May we resolve enmity and dispel grudges;
May we distance ourselves from ignorance;
May we be completely understand the Dharma;
May we not create distressing causes.

Oh great, compassionate Buddha!
We would like to express gratitude
For the compassion of all Buddhas and bodhisattvas:
Since the past kalpa,
All beings have been lost in the abyss of the karma of wrongdoings.
It is the Dharma that teaches and guides us in the method of repentance,
It is the Dharma water that cleanses our karma of enmity.

Oh great, compassionate Buddha!
We would like to embody the compassion and wisdom
Of all Buddhas and bodhisattvas;
We would like to emulate the actions and vows

祈求您以佛光加被我們——
　　讓我們不要隨順惡業，讓我們不要再造新殃，
　　讓我們不要違背因果，讓我們不要忘失信心。
祈求您以慈雲覆護我們——
　　讓我們能夠解冤釋結，讓我們能夠遠離無明，
　　讓我們能夠具足佛法，讓我們能夠不造苦因。

慈悲偉大的佛陀！
我們要感恩諸佛菩薩的慈悲，
曠劫以來，
眾生迷失於罪業深淵之中，
　　是佛法，教導懺悔的法門，
　　是法水，洗滌我們的冤業。

慈悲偉大的佛陀！
我們要以諸佛菩薩的悲智為榜樣，

Of ancient virtuous and wise ones;
We would like to exalt the method of the repentance service
To enable everyone to cleanse themselves of the karma of wrongdoings,
And move towards a happy life;
We would like to repent for the masses everywhere,
To enable them to take the precious raft of the Dharma
Across the sea of suffering to liberation together.

Oh great, compassionate Buddha,
Please accept my sincerest prayer!
Oh great, compassionate Buddha,
Please accept my sincerest prayer!

我們要以古聖先賢的行願為典範。
我們要發揚懺悔的法門,
　讓大家洗清罪業,
　走向幸福的人生;
我們要代十方大眾懺悔,
　讓大家共乘寶筏,
　同登解脫的彼岸。

慈悲偉大的佛陀!
祈求您接受我至誠的祈願,
慈悲偉大的佛陀!
祈求您接受我至誠的祈願。

A Prayer for the Yogacara Dharma Service

Oh great, compassionate Buddha!
The causal condition of the hungry ghost "Flaming Mouth"
Caused you to proclaim for Venerable Elder Ananda
The method of bestowing food to hungry ghosts;
Through reciting the dharani,
You transformed drops of water into a river of milk,
And changed particles into bushels of food for the great earth;
Then, suddenly,
You relieved famine everywhere in the world;
In an instant,
You benefited the destiny of countless hungry ghosts.
From that moment on,
All the hungry ghosts have had the hope of being rescued.

Oh great, compassionate Buddha!
Hungry ghosts are some of the most miserable beings:
In their world,
Sunshine has disappeared;
Gentle breezes no longer caress;
The whole earth is a desolate wasteland;
Streams are filled with pus and blood.

焰口祈願文

慈悲偉大的佛陀！
　由於您藉面然鬼王的緣起，
為阿難尊者宣說施食的方法，
　以陀羅尼真言，
化滴水作長河之酥酪，
變微粒為大地之斛食，
　於倏忽間，普濟大地之饑虛；
在頃刻時，利益河沙之鬼趣。
餓鬼眾生從此有了得救的希望。

慈悲偉大的佛陀！
　餓鬼是最悲苦的眾生之一，
在他們的世界裡，
陽光已經隱沒，和風不再吹拂，
土地都是荒漠，溪流充滿膿血。

Some of them spit out blazing flames
That burn fiercely without ceasing;
Some of them have a belly as large as a mountain,
And a throat as narrow as a needle;
Some of them have a foul odor in their mouths
And often vomit;
Some of them have sharp body hair,
And suffer unbearable pain.
They endure unbearable hunger and thirst for months and years;
They are in the stage between death and rebirth, and wander everywhere;
Their appearance is emaciated and is feared by all;
Their hair is in disarray;
They hide during the day and come out at night.

Oh Buddha!
We pray to you to cover and protect them with clouds of compassion:
Please always let their throats open
And be smooth and supple;
Please let their food and drink be sufficient,
And let them always be full;
Please let them have a stable residence,
And no longer wander about;

他們有的口吐烈焰，熾然不熄；
他們有的腹大如山，咽細如針；
他們有的口中惡臭，經常嘔逆；
他們有的身毛堅利，痛苦不堪；
　他們經年累月，饑渴難耐；
　他們中陰為身，到處飄泊；
　他們形容枯槁，人見人畏；
　他們頭髮散亂，晝伏夜行。

啊！佛陀！
祈求您以慈雲覆護他們，
　讓他們咽喉常開，通順流暢；
　讓他們飲食具足，經常飽滿；
　讓他們居有定所，不再飄盪；

Please let their vexation and suffering be alleviated,
And let them be reborn in the upper realms soon.

Oh great, compassionate Buddha!
All beings in the hungry ghost realm
Are the result of the retribution of karma:
Some of them are there because of killing, stealing, and sexual misconduct;
Some of them are there because of the karma created by speech;
Some of them are there because of anger and ignorance;
Some of them are there because of obtaining wealth by unjust means.

Oh Buddha!
We pray to you to bless them with your Buddha light:
May they understand cause and effect,
And correct the past and cultivate the future;
May they know how to repent
And cultivate merits and wisdom;
May they take refuge in the Triple Gem,
And break away from the lower realms;
May they rise to heavenly or human realms,
And enjoy wonderful happiness.

讓他們減少憂苦,早日超生。

慈悲偉大的佛陀!
餓鬼道的眾生也是業報所成,
他們有的是因為殺盜邪淫,
他們有的是因為口舌造業,
他們有的是因為瞋恚愚癡,
他們有的是因為貪贓枉法。

啊!佛陀!
祈求您以佛光加被他們,
讓他們明白因果,改往修來;
讓他們懂得懺悔,修福修慧;
讓他們皈依三寶,早離惡道;
讓他們得昇人天,受勝妙樂。

Oh great, compassionate Buddha!
In the human world,
There are also many people who entertain sinister schemes:
They do not attend to a legitimate profession, and do harm everywhere;
They are perverse and recalcitrant and act criminally;
They create rumors, incite incidents, and subvert society;
They exploit others' possessions, and embezzle public funds.

Oh Buddha!
These evil people in the human world
Are at times more terrifying than ghosts;
These evil people in the human world
Are at times more brutal than ghosts.

Oh great, compassionate Buddha,
As the ghosts in the underworld surely need to be raised
From the lower realms to the upper ones;
So the ghosts in the human world
Also need to be rescued.
We pray to you to bless them:
Please grant them the causes and conditions

慈悲偉大的佛陀！
人間也有許多心懷鬼胎的人，
　　他們不務正業，到處為害；
　　他們邪僻乖張，作奸犯科；
　　他們造謠生事，顛覆社會；
　　他們剝削他有，飽入私囊。

佛陀！
　　人間的歹徒有時比鬼怪還要恐怖，
　　人間的邪惡有時比鬼怪還要狠毒。

慈悲偉大的佛陀！
陰間的鬼固然要去超薦，
　　人間的鬼也有待度化。
祈求您加被他們，
　　賜給他們察覺過失的因緣，

To become aware of their mistakes;
Please grant them the opportunity
To turn over a new leaf;
May this mundane world also be like the Pure Land,
Where there is no name for the lower realms,
But only meeting places for benevolent people.

Oh great, compassionate Buddha,
Please accept our sincerest prayer!
Oh great, compassionate Buddha,
Please accept our sincerest prayer!

賜給他們重新做人的機會；
希望娑婆世界也能如淨土一樣，
　沒有惡道的名稱，
　都是善人的會所。

慈悲偉大的佛陀！
請您接受我至誠的祈願！
慈悲偉大的佛陀！
請您接受我至誠的祈願！

A Prayer for Pilgrimage

Oh great, compassionate Buddha!
The sound of the bell slices the silent sky;
The wooden fish matches the sound of the Buddhist
        hymns.
Today, we approach you in a very sincere state of mind,
In pilgrimage before your sacred image,
To worship your golden body.
We, of one heart and mind, chant your name;
We prostrate ourselves with the utmost sincerity before
        you.
In an instant, we discard all distracting thoughts and
        wild ideas behind us;
In an instant, we completely remove arrogant egotism.
Our pulse begins to echo with yours,
Our minds gradually blend with yours.

Oh our respected and beloved Buddha!
Let us pull up the screens of selfishness;
Let us put down the arrogant curtain of pride;
Let us cooperate with each other;
Let us achieve the Buddha Way together.

朝山祈願文

慈悲偉大的佛陀！
　鐘聲劃破寂靜的天空，
　木魚和著梵唱的音聲，
我們今天懷著懇切的心情，
　來朝拜您的聖容，來禮敬您的金身。
我們一心一意的稱念聖號，
我們五體投地的頂禮佛足。
　頓時，把雜念妄想拋在腦後，
　頓時，把貢高我慢一掃而光。
我們的脈搏開始與您呼應，
我們的心靈逐漸與您融和。

我們所敬愛的佛陀啊！
　讓我們拉起自私的簾幕，
　讓我們放下驕傲的慢幢，
　讓我們互相提攜，
　讓我們共成佛道。

Oh great, compassionate Buddha!
The gentle breeze blows calmly,
The incense cloud is present all around;
Today, we approach you in a very sincere state of mind,
In pilgrimage before your sacred image,
To worship your golden body.
We are not afraid of the sand and stone on the road,
Nor the heavy dew on the journey,
But only of our inability to eliminate our karmic hindrances,
Our inability to completely wash away our disgraceful wrongdoings.

Oh Buddha, whom we turn to and rely on:
Please let us purify the karma operating in our body, speech, and mind;
Please let us increase the cultivation of precepts, meditation, and wisdom;
Please let us cross the sea of suffering safely;
Please let us arrive at Buddhas' lands smoothly.

Oh great, compassionate Buddha!
The filthy atmosphere disappears in a glance, and
The pure and clean temple appears right before us;

慈悲偉大的佛陀！
　　和風徐徐地吹起，
　　香雲彌漫在四周，
我們今天懷著懺悔的心情，
　　來朝拜您的聖容，來禮敬您的金身。
不怕路上砂石多，
不怕途中露水重，
　　只怕我們的業障無法消除，
　　只怕我們的罪垢無法滌盡。

我們所皈依的佛陀啊！
請讓我們清淨身口意業，
請讓我們增上戒定慧學，
　　讓我們平安地越過苦海，
　　讓我們順利地到達佛國。

慈悲偉大的佛陀！
　　污煙瘴氣在眼底消失，
　　清淨梵刹在面前出現，

Today, we approach you in a state of mind that longs for the Way,
In pilgrimage before your dignified image,
To worship your golden body.
We prostrate ourselves
From the bottom to the top of the hill,
From outside the gate to inside the temple;
The more we prostrate ourselves,
The higher we climb, the closer we come before you.
Oh, our most admired and respected Buddha:
We are merely ordinary people,
We are merely beginning Buddhists;
We are willing to take the spirit of the Buddha as a model,
To awaken self and others;
We are willing to follow the steps of the Buddha
To benefit self and others.

Oh great, compassionate Buddha!
The polluted, mundane world is put behind us,
The pure, cool Dharma-water cleanses our body and mind.
Today, we approach you in a state of mind of zealous progress,
In pilgrimage to your dignified face,
To worship your golden body.

我們今天懷著慕道的心情，
　　來朝拜您的聖容，來禮敬您的金身。
我們從山下拜到山上，
我們從門外拜到殿內，
我們越拜越往高處攀昇，
我們越拜越近您的座前，
我們最景仰的佛陀啊！
　　我們只是凡夫俗子，
　　我們只是初學行者，
我們願效法佛陀的精神，自覺覺他；
我們願追隨佛陀的腳步，自利利人。

慈悲偉大的佛陀！
　　污染的紅塵遠拋在身後，
　　清涼的法水沐浴著身心。
我們今天懷著精進的心情，
　　來朝拜您的聖容，
　　來禮敬您的金身。

We are not afraid of the long journey,
Nor of the difficult mountain path;
We finally arrive before you,
We finally kneel before you.

Our respected and beloved Buddha!
With your prayer,
Please protect us in welcoming your brightness;
Please support us in marching towards the great bodhi way.

Oh great, compassionate Buddha,
Please accept our sincerest prayer!
Oh great, compassionate Buddha,
Please accept our sincerest prayer!

不懼路途遙遠，不畏山徑難行，
　我們終於來到了您的座前，
　我們終於匍匐在您的腳下。

我們所尊敬的佛陀啊！
請庇佑我們不斷迎向光明，
請加持我們邁向菩提大道。

慈悲偉大的佛陀！
請您接受我至誠的祈願！
慈悲偉大的佛陀！
請您接受我至誠的祈願！

A Prayer for Deities and Ghosts

Oh great, compassionate Buddha!
Today we would like to pray to you for deities and ghosts.
Although they cannot be felt or touched by ordinary human beings,
They still live in the same dharma realms;
They have even once been born into the human realm,
And have been born as our parents and relatives in former lives:
Some of them have been nobility, and military and political leaders;
Some of them have been people of the lower classes;
Some of them have been very wealthy business magnates;
Some of them have been poor scholars;
Some of them have been faithful, honest women of virtuous upbringing;
Some of them have been heroes and outstanding people;
Some of them have been gifted scholars and beautiful ladies;
Some of them have been fortune-tellers and practitioners of divination.

為神鬼靈祇祈願文

慈悲偉大的佛陀!
　我今天要為神鬼靈祇向您祈願。
　他們雖非凡夫肉軀所能感觸,
　但也同樣生活在法界之內,
甚至,
他們曾經生於人道,
他們曾經是
　我們宿世的父母宗親:
他們有的曾經是王侯將相,
他們有的曾經是販夫走卒,
他們有的曾經是萬貫巨賈,
他們有的曾經是窮苦書生,
他們有的曾經是忠良烈女,
他們有的曾經是英雄豪傑,
他們有的曾經是才子佳人,
他們有的曾經是占星卜士。

No matter whether they were filled with good fortune,
Or burdened with unwholesome karma,
As deities and ghosts they still possess the feelings of
      joy, anger, sorrow, and happiness;
They still possess love, hatred, passion, and enmity;
They still possess greed, anger, suspicion, and jealousy;
They still possess ignorance and delusions.
Therefore,
Although they have supernatural power,
They are still not at ease;
Although they have strong force,
They still do not have complete comprehension of truth.

Oh great, compassionate Buddha!
"All beings possess the Buddha Nature,
"All beings are able to attain enlightenment."
We pray for the support of your great power to allow
      them to:
Take refuge in the Triple Gem;
Repent the karma of past wrongdoings,
And transform delusion into enlightenment;
Raise to heavenly or human realms
And enjoy victorious, wonderful ease and joy;
Study and cultivate the Dharma
And reject unreal and false ideas;

不管是善福滿盈，或是惡業纏身，
作為神鬼靈祇，
    他們有喜怒哀樂，
    他們有愛恨情仇，
甚至，
    他們也有貪瞋疑嫉，
    他們也有愚癡無明。
所以，
    他們雖有神通，但不自在；
    他們縱有勢力，也不究竟。

慈悲偉大的佛陀！
「眾生皆有佛性，眾生皆能得度。」
    祈求您的大力加被，
    讓他們都能皈投在三寶座下，
懺除往昔罪業，
    轉迷情為悟者；
超升人天善道，
    享受勝妙安樂；
修習佛法真諦，

Have their minds opened and liberated
To foster good causes and conditions of blessed virtues.
Like Sakra Devanamindra,
Who studied the Dharma and protected Buddhism;
As a result, he removed unwholesome karma
And was raised to the heavenly realm;
Like Hariti,
Who was once addicted to stealing and eating children's flesh,
Who was converted by Sakyamuni, obtained merits, and became a protectoress of Buddhism;
Like Drumakimnara-Raja, a musician,
Who used music to help propagate Buddhism
And gained respect from tens of thousands of people;
Like Pisaca, head of the demons,
Who used supernatural power
To protect all beings and attained the Buddha's praise.
They have set an example for deities and ghosts,
They have left instructive anecdotes
For all beings of future generations.

Oh great, compassionate Buddha!
Please protect all deities and ghosts.
Under your reception and guidance:

捨除虛妄顛倒；
獲得心開意解，
　培植福德因緣。
像帝釋天因為學佛護法，
　捨除惡業而上昇天界；
像鬼子母原本嗜食血肉，
　因痛改前罪而獲得福報；
像大樹緊那羅以音樂助佛法化，
　受到萬千眾生的禮敬；
像大自在鬼王以神力護衛眾生，
　得到佛陀的嘉許授記。
他們為神鬼靈祇立下了榜樣，
他們為後世眾生留下了美談。

慈悲偉大的佛陀！
祈求您庇佑所有的神鬼靈祇，
讓他們在您的接引下，

May they all initiate the bodhi mind
To carry out the bodhisattva path;
May they be compassionate and joy-giving
To benefit self and others;
May they all follow what their circumstances are
To receive and convert the same beings;
May they all strengthen their actions and vows
To enrich all beings.
In the future world:
May there be no suffering or lower realms;
May all virtuous people come together in one place;
May the pure land be present before us.

Oh great, compassionate Buddha,
Please accept our sincerest prayer!
Oh great, compassionate Buddha,
Please accept our sincerest prayer!

都能發菩提心，行菩薩道；
都能慈悲喜捨，自利利他；
都能隨所在處，攝化同類；
都能堅固行願，饒益眾生。
希望未來的世間，
　　無諸憂苦，惡道除名，
　　善人聚會，淨土現前。

慈悲偉大的佛陀！
請求您接受我至誠的祈願。
慈悲偉大的佛陀！
請求您接受我至誠的祈願。

Endnotes and Glossary

註解與名相解說

Endnotes

1. *Cross-Island Highway in Taiwan* — Approximately 117 miles in length; this highway links Taiwan's east and west coasts, crossing some of Taiwan's most rugged mountains.

2. *Three Gorges of the Yangtze River* — The three Yangtze River gorges are the Qutang Gorge, Wu Gorge, and Xiling Gorge, collectively known as the Sanxia, or "The Three Gorges." They are located in between Fengjei, Sichun Province and Yichang, Hubei Province.

3. *Imperial Tsing Ma Bridge* — With a single span of 4,475 feet and an overall length of 1.3 miles, it is the second-longest suspension bridge in the world; it was completed in 1997.

4. *Mei Lanfang* — (1894-1961 C.E.), a Peking opera performer, internationally famous for his portrayals of female characters.

5. *Bruce Lee* — (1940-1973 C.E.), also known as Lee Hsiao Lung; famous in Chinese martial arts.

6. *Ling Po* — Born in 1939 C.E. One of her most famous Huangmei melodies is "The Love Story of Liang Shanbo and Zhu Yingtai" (1963).

7. *Yang Lihua* — Born in 1944 C.E. She played an important role in the movement to improve the Taiwanese folk opera.

註 解

1. 台灣橫貫公路 — 全長約195公里，連接台灣的東岸和西岸，跨越了台灣最峻峭的山脈。

2. 長江三峽 — 指瞿塘峽、巫峽和西陵峽。位於四川奉節縣和湖北宜昌縣間。

3. 青衣大橋 — 單長約4,475英呎，全長1.3英哩。它為世界上第二長的大橋。

4. 梅蘭芳 — 西元1894至1961年，北京京劇家，因反串角色而著名於世。

5. 李小龍 — 西元1940至1973年，以功夫享譽影壇。

6. 凌波 — 生於西元1939年，她最為著名的黃梅調之一是「梁山伯與祝英台」。

7. 楊麗花 — 生於西元1944年。她在推動和改進台灣歌仔戲的運動中扮演一個非常重要的角色。

8. *Sai Jinhua* — (1875-1937 C.E.), she saved many lives during the events of the Boxer Rebellion and the Invasions of Eight Powers.

9. *The Boxer Rebellion* — A religious, anti-foreign uprising in China in 1900. "The Boxers" believed that Westerners were out to destroy traditional Chinese culture.

10. *The Invasions of Eight Powers* — The invasion of China by the United Kingdom, Russia, France, German, Italy, Japan, the United States, and Austria.

11. *Cai Songpo* — (1882-1916 C.E.), also known as Cai Er.

12. *Yuan Shikai* — (1859-1916 C.E.), the first president of the Republic of China, who died shortly after he proclaimed himself emperor.

13. *Amra Garden* — Located in the City of Vaisali, India.

14. *Vasumitra* — She attained the state of purification of "the greedy desires," and she taught this Dharma method of purification to others.

15. *Wen Tianxiang* — (1236-1283 C.E.), the last prime minister of the Chinese Song Dynasty, who was executed by the Mongolians.

16. *Shi Kefa* — (1604-1645 C.E.), a famous general who served at

8. 賽金花 — 西元1875至1937年。在義和團事件和八國聯軍中，救了許多人的性命。

9. 義和團 — 一個宗教組織，深信西方人會破壞中國的傳統，所以倡言扶清滅洋。

10. 八國聯軍 — 指英、俄、法、德、義、日、美、奧等八國共組聯軍攻華。

11. 蔡松坡 — 西元1882至1916年，又名蔡鍔。

12. 袁世凱 — 西元1859至1916年，中華民國第一任總統，死於自行稱帝後不久。

13. 庵摩羅園 — 位於印度舍聲城。

14. 婆須蜜多 — 她已達到離貪的清淨境界，也因此教大眾此法門。

15. 文天祥 — 西元1236至1283年，宋朝最後一位丞相，最後被元兵處決。

16. 史可法 — 西元1604至1645年，明朝末年，滿清入侵中

the end of the Chinese Ming Dynasty; he opposed the Manchu Army when the Manchus invaded the Central Plain of China.

17. *Guan Yu* — (?-219 C.E.), also known as the "Guardian of Warriors" in China.

18. *Yue Fei* — (1103-1142 C.E.), a famous general, who opposed the Jin Army in the Chinese Southern Song Dynasty.

19. *Mount Hiei* — Located in Shiga Prefecture (near Kyoto) in Japan; the center of the Tendai School in Japanese Buddhism.

20. *Baizhang* — (720-814 C.E.), also known as "Baizhang Huaihai"; a master in the Chinese Tang Dynasty, who established the system in which the Sangha provides its own daily necessities by cultivating vegetables. This kind of system is called "the monastic regulations of Baizhang" (Ch. Baizhang Qing Gui).

21. *Daoxuan* – (596-667 C.E.), a Vinaya master in the Chinese Tang Dynasty; the founder of the Nanshan Vinaya School.

22. *Jianzhen* — (687-763 C.E.), a master in the Chinese Tang Dynasty, who brought Vinaya to Japan; known as the First Patriarch of the Vinaya School in Japanese Buddhism.

23. *Pei Xiu* — A prime minister in China's Tang Dynasty, who supported Buddhism (when Buddhism was being suppressed) dur-

原時的一位名將。

17. 關羽(關雲長) — 卒於西元219年，被譽為中國戰神。

18. 岳飛(岳武穆) — 西元1103至1142年，南宋時抗金名將。

19. 比郁山 — 位於日本近江國滋賀郡，為日本天台宗的大山。

20. 百丈 — 西元720至814年，又稱百丈懷海，為僧團建自給自足的農禪生活，世稱百丈清規。

21. 道宣 — 西元596至667年，唐朝律僧，南山律宗的祖。

22. 鑑真 — 西元687至763年，唐朝僧。攜帶戒律渡海到本，為日本律宗的始祖。

23. 斐休 — 唐朝宰相。在武、宣宗時，佛教遭難，出而護。

ing the reigns of Emperor Wuzong and Emperor Xuanzong.

24. *Yang Renshan* – (1837-1911 C.E.), also known as Yang Wenhui, who was the central figure in the reform movement of Chinese Buddhism at the end of the Chinese Qing Dynasty.

25. *Lu Bicheng* — (1886-1946 C.E.), who translated the English-Chinese edition of the "Chapter of the Universal Gateway" of the *Lotus Sutra*.

26. *Sun Qingyang* — (1913 -), an important figure among the lay people in recent Chinese Buddhism, who assisted Master Taixu in developing modern Chinese Buddhism. He supported the printing of *The Buddhist Canon* (Ch. Da Zheng Zang.)

27. *Daoan* — A great master in the Chinese Eastern Jin Dynasty, who contributed highly to the translation and interpretation of sutras.

28. *Mahinda* — A son of King Asoka; the founder of Sri Lankan Buddhism, and also known as "the Sixth Patriarch of the Vinaya School."

29. *Sanghamitta* — A daughter of King Asoka, who brought the seeds of the bodhi tree to Sri Lanka.

30. *Kuiji* — (632-682 C.E.), a Chan master in the Chinese Tang

24. 楊仁山 — 西元1837至1911年，又名楊文會。為清末復興中國佛教的樞紐人物。

25. 呂碧城 — 西元1886至1946年，曾譯中英對照的法華經普門品。

26. 孫清揚 — 中國近代佛教上，著名的在家居士。他曾協助太虛大師發展近代中國佛教和編印大正藏。

27. 道安 — 東晉高僧，對於譯經及經典注釋，具有卓越貢獻。

28. 摩哂陀 — 阿育王之子，錫蘭佛教的創始者，也被稱為律宗的第六祖。

29. 僧伽密多 — 阿育王之女，曾帶菩提葉的種子到錫蘭。

30. 窺基 — 西元632至682年，唐代僧，玄奘大師的弟子，

Dynasty, one of disciples of Master Xuanzang, and the founder of the Cien School of Buddhism.

31. *Jizang* — (549-623 C.E.), a master in the Chinese Sui Dynasty, also known as "Master Jiaxiang."

32. *Yitian* — (1055-1101 C.E.), also known as Chan Master Dajue. He went to China to study the Dharma, and later he greatly contributed to the compilation of *The Buddhist Canon*.

33. *Huike* — (487-593 C.E.), a Chan master during the Chinese Southern and Northern Dynasties. He studied the Dharma under Master Bodhidharma's instruction, and later he became the Second Patriarch of the Chan School.

34. *Fayuan* — (991-1067 C.E.), a Chan master of the Linji School in the Chinese Song Dynasty; also known as "Fushan Jiudai."

35. *Beidu* — (?-426 C.E.), a Chan master in the Chinese Jin Dynasty.

36. *Yiyuan* — (1592-1673 C.E.), also known as "Longqi." He was a Chan master in the Chinese Ming Dynasty, and founder of the Obaku-shu School in Japan.

37. *Zhongfeng* — A Chan master of the Linji School of Buddhism during the Chinese Yuan Dynasty.

38. *Ajatasatru* — In the Buddha's time, he was a king of the Magadha Kingdom. He killed his father, King Bimbisara, in order to inherit the throne. Later, he repented for murdering his father and became a follower of the Buddha.

39. *Yuan Liaofan* — (1533-1606 C.E.), a famous Confucian scholar in the Chinese Ming Dynasty. In middle-age, after he met Chan Master Yungu Hui, he became a devout Buddhist and diligently practiced the Dharma. He wrote one book, entitled *Liao Fan's Four Lessons*.

38. 阿闍世王 —— 佛陀時代，摩揭陀國的國王，殺父篡位。後來懺悔其過，並皈依佛陀。

39. 袁了凡 —— 西元1533至1606年，明代著名的儒士，後遇雲谷會禪師，變成佛教徒，精進道業，改變際遇。著有「了凡四訓」一書。

Glossary

Amitabha Buddha: Presides over the Pure Land of the West; also known as "the Buddha of Infinite Light" and "the Buddha of Infinite Life."

Avalokitesvara Bodhisattva: Literally, "the one who hears the sounds of the world." In Mahayana Buddhism, Avalokitesvara is known as the Bodhisattva of Compassion. He can manifest himself in any form necessary in order to help any being. Widely revered in China as Kuan Yin Bodhisattva.

Bodhi: It means "awakened" or "enlightened," and refers to the wisdom that eliminates all afflictions and delusions, and leads one towards liberation.

Bodhi mind: Skt. "bodhicitta"; also known as "anuttara-samyak-sambodhi"; refers to the mind seeking to achieve enlightenment. It is the basis for all Buddhas to attain Buddhahood. If one bears this kind of mind and diligently cultivates oneself, one will surely attain enlightenment. Therefore, bodhi mind is the foundation of all correct vows, the basis of enlightenment, and the foundation of great compassion and the bodhisattva path.

Buddha: Literally, "the awakened one" or "the enlightened one," who has attained enlightenment, liberated sentient beings, and

名相解說

阿彌陀佛：西方極樂世界的教主，阿彌陀，又意譯為「無量光」、「無量壽」。

觀音：即為「觀世音菩薩」，以慈悲救濟眾生為本願之菩薩，凡遇難眾生誦其名號，菩薩即時觀其音聲前往拯救，故稱「觀世音」。

菩提：意譯為「覺」、「知」，乃指斷絕煩惱而成就涅槃的智慧。

菩提心：梵語bodhicitta，全稱阿耨多羅三藐三菩提，此為一切諸佛之種子，若發起此心勤行精進，當得速成無上菩提。故知菩提心乃一切正願之始、菩提之根本、大悲及菩薩學之所依。

佛：意譯「覺者」、「知者」。意即具足自覺、覺他、

achieved the perfection of all practices. Here, "Buddha" refers to the historical Buddha, Sakyamuni Buddha.

Buddha Nature: The inherent nature that exists in all beings. It is the capability to achieve Buddhahood.

Buddhas' lands: Refers to the lands where Buddhas preside or the places where they expound the Dharma.

Causes and conditions: Skt. "hetu-pratyaya." "Hetu" means the cause, or direct reason, for a particular phenomenon. "Pratyaya" is translated as condition, or the indirect causes of a phenomenon, resulting from external circumstance. The arising and extinction of all phenomena are due to causes and conditions.

Cause and Effect: Skt. "hetu-phala." This is the most basic doctrine in Buddhism, which explains all the relations and connections of all phenomena in the world. This law means that the arising of each and every phenomenon is due to its own causes and conditions, and the actual form, or appearance, of all phenomena is the effect.

Dharma: Refers to the ultimate Truth, and the teachings of the Buddha.

覺行圓滿之大聖者。本文裡，指的是釋迦牟尼佛。

真如自性：指佛的本性，或指成佛的可能性，而一切眾生皆有此本質。

佛國：指佛所住之處，或佛教化之國土。

因緣：梵語hetupratyaya為因與緣之並稱。因，指引生結果之直接原因；緣，指由外來相助之間接緣因。一切萬有皆由因緣之聚散而生滅。

因果：梵語hetuphala，為佛教教義體系中，用來說明世界一切關係之基本理論。一切諸法之形成，因為能生，果為所生。

法：指真理或是佛陀的教示。

Dharma-body: Or "Dharmakaya." It indicates the Dharma taught by the Buddha or the Truth realized by the Buddha. It also refers to the true nature of the Buddha or the unity of the Buddha with all phenomena.

Dharani: Literally this word means "uniting and upholding." It refers to the wisdom to remember, unify, and uphold the immeasurable Dharma without forgetting. Later, it became an epithet meaning "spell."

Dravya: (Full name: "Dravya-malla-putra.") He was one of the Buddha's disciples who became a novice monk at the age of fourteen and attained arhatship at sixteen. He was good at making tools, building houses, and general construction.

Five desires: Indicates the desires of 1) wealth, beauty, fame, food, and sleep, or 2) form, sound, fragrance, taste, and touch.

Five precepts: Indicates no killing, no stealing, no sexual misconduct, no lying, and no taking of intoxicants.

Four means of embracing: Indicates four methods that bodhisattvas use to guide sentient beings to the path of liberation. They are: 1) give charity, 2) utter kind words, 3) act altruistically and beneficently, and 4) cooperate and adapt oneself to others.

法身：指佛所說之正法，佛所得之無漏法，即佛之自性真如如來藏。

陀羅尼：梵語之音譯，意譯為總持。即能總攝憶持無量佛法而不忘失之念慧力。後世與咒混同，統稱咒語為陀羅尼。

陀羅驃：全名Dravyamallaputra，為佛陀的弟子，十四歲出家，十六歲證得阿羅漢果。善長於修造工具，安造房舍。

五欲：指財欲、色欲、飲食欲、名欲、睡眠欲；或色欲、聲欲、香欲、味欲、觸欲。

五戒：不殺生、不偷盜、不邪淫、不妄語、不飲酒。

四攝：即菩薩攝受眾生，令其開悟的四種方法，即為布施、愛語、利行、同事。、

Good Dharma friends: Indicates the virtuous ones who can guide people to the right path.

Karmic hindrances: Skt. "karmavarana." Since all intentional actions or deeds produce effects, bad conduct results in bad karmic effects and thus hinders our way to enlightenment.

Ksitigarbha Bodhisattva: One of the great bodhisattvas in Mahayana Buddhism. He vowed not to attain Buddhahood until all sentient beings in hell are liberated.

Loving-kindness, compassion, joy, and equanimity: Also known as "the four immeasurable states of mind."

Maudgalyayana: One of the Buddha's ten great disciples. He is well-known as the foremost in supernatural powers.

Mundane (Saha) world: Also known as "Endurance world." It indicates the present world in which we reside, full of suffering to be endured. The beings in this world endure suffering and affliction due to their greed, anger, and ignorance.

Nagarjuna Bodhisattva: He is the founder of the Madhyamika School (the Middle School) of Buddhism, and the author of many commentaries and treatises. His famous works include *Treatise on the Perfection of Great Wisdom, Treatise on the*

善知識：指正直有德行的人，能教導正道之人。

業障：梵語karmavarana。所有的行為活動都會產生果報，而惡行會產生惡業，而惡業能蔽障正道，故稱業障。

地藏菩薩：大乘佛教的著名菩薩之一。他曾發願地獄不空，誓不成佛的偉大誓願。

慈悲喜捨：又稱四無量心。

目犍連：十大弟子之一，被譽稱為神通第一。

娑婆世界：又稱「堪忍世界」，指我們人所住的世界。此世界充滿痛苦，而此世界的眾生安於忍受痛苦煩惱，而不肯出離，故名「堪忍」。

龍樹菩薩：中觀學派的創始者，著有大智度論、中觀論等。也因此被譽為千部論師。

Middle Path, and many more. Therefore, he was given the title of "Master of a Thousand Commentaries."

Nalanda: Located in Baragaon, close to Bajgir, India. In the early fifth century, King Sakraditya built this temple. It was the largest monastery and university in ancient India, and also a center of the Mind-Only School and Tantric Buddhism.

Noble Eightfold Path: Indicates right view, right thought, right speech, right action, right livelihood, right effort, right mindfulness, and right meditative concentration.

Prajna wisdom: Skt. "prajna" means wisdom. It is one of six paramitas, known as "the Mother of all Buddhas," and also the basis of the other five paramitas. See *six perfections*.

Pure Land: Refers to the realm where Buddhas reside, or the purified place built upon the power of cultivating bodhi.

Pure Land of the East: Indicates the Pure Land of the Medicine Buddha, built upon the power of the Medicine Buddha's "twelve great vows."

Pure Land of Ultimate Bliss: It usually indicates the Pure Land of the West, where Amitabha Buddha presides.

那爛陀：位於今日印度的八達加歐之靠近拉察基爾。五世紀出，為帝日王興建此寺，它為古印度時佛教最大寺院及學府，也為唯識學派及密教之一的大中心。

八正道：正見、正思惟、正語、正業、正命、正精進、正念、正定。

般若：梵語paramita意譯為慧、智，為六波羅蜜之一，被稱為「諸佛之母」，為其他五波羅蜜的根據。

淨土：指以菩提修成之清淨處所，為佛所居之所。

琉璃淨土：指藥師如來的淨土，以藥師如來的十二大願所建立。

極樂淨土：通常指西方極樂世界，阿彌陀佛為西方淨土的教主。

Purna: In Pali, "Punna," one of the ten great disciples of the Buddha and known as the foremost in preaching the Dharma.

Sangha: One of three elements of the Triple Gem; refers to monastics or the community of Buddhist disciples.

Sariputra: He was one of the Buddha's ten great disciples and well known as the foremost in wisdom.

Sentient beings: Skt. "sattvas"; refers to beings with consciousness, including the celestial beings, asuras, humans, animals, hungry ghosts, and hellish beings.

Six perfections: Also known as "six paramitas." The six perfections include the perfections of giving charity, upholding precepts, patience, diligence, meditative concentration, and wisdom.

Six points of reverent harmony: Indicates 1) physical unity by living together, 2) verbal unity by not criticizing others, 3) mental unity through shared joy, 4) moral unity through upholding the same precepts, 5) doctrinal unity in views, and 6) eco-

富樓那：巴利名為 Punna，佛陀的十大弟子之一，被譽為說法第一。

僧伽：三寶之一；指出家人或指信受佛法，修行佛道之團體。

舍利佛：佛陀十大弟子之一，被譽為智慧第一。

眾生：梵語sattva，意指有情識眾生，包括天人、阿修羅、人、畜生、餓鬼、地獄道眾生。

六波羅蜜：指布施、持戒、忍辱、精進、禪定、智慧。

六合敬：指身合敬、口合敬、意合敬、戒合敬、見合敬、利合敬。

nomic unity through sharing.

Six sense-organs: Indicates eyes, ears, nose, tongue, body, and mind.

Srimala: The daughter of King Prasenajit of the Kausala Kingdom. Because she was influenced by her parents, she took refuge in the Triple Gem. She also received the Buddha's prophecy of her attainment of Buddhahood because of her respect, and praises to the Tathagata.

Sudatta: The name "Sudatta" means "Well-giving." He was an elder of the City of Sravasti, an administrator of King Prasenajit. He was also known as "Anathapindana." After taking refuge in the Buddha, he built the Jetavana Grove for the Buddha to give discourses on the Dharma and for the gathering of the Sangha.

Supernatural Powers: In Buddhism, there are six kinds — the supernatural powers of psychic traveling, clairaudience (deva-ear), clairvoyance (deva-eye), mental telepathy, knowledge of past and future, and ending contamination.

Take refuge in the Triple Gem: Taking refuge in the Buddha, the Dharma, and the Sangha.

Ten directions: In Buddhism, this term is used to refer to "everywhere," indicating the eight points of the compass (north,

六根：指眼、耳、鼻、舌、身、意。

勝鬘夫人：舍衛國波斯匿王之女。因受父母之薰陶而皈依佛道，敬禮讚歎如來，得當來受作佛之授記。

須達長者：梵語 Sudatta 意譯為善施。他為舍衛城的長者，波斯匿王的大臣。人稱他為給孤獨長者 (Anathapindana)。皈依佛陀後，建造祇園精舍 (Jetavana Grove)供養佛陀。

神通：佛教裡有六種神通，它們為神足通、天耳通、天眼通、他心通、宿命通、漏盡通。

三皈：皈依佛，皈依法，皈依僧。

十方：指東、西、南、北、東南、西南、東北、西

west, east, south, southeast, southwest, northeast and northwest) plus the zenith and nadir.

Ten wholesome conducts: Indicates no killing, no stealing, no sexual misconduct, no lying, no duplicity, no harsh words, no flattery, no greed, no hatred (or anger), and no ignorance.

The Medicine Buddha: The Buddha who presides over the Pure Land of the East, based on the power of his twelve great vows to achieve Buddhahood.

Three great kalpas: A measuring unit of time in ancient India, a kalpa is an immense and inconceivable length of time. Buddhism adapts it to refer to the period of time between the creation and recreation of the worlds. The three great kalpas refer to the period of time beween the great vow made by a bodhisattva to achieve Buddhahood, and the fulfillment of that vow.

Three poisons: Indicates greed, anger, and ignorance.

Three Studies: Indicates the precepts, meditation, and wisdom.

Triple Gem: Indicates the Buddha, the Dharma, and the Sangha.

Vimalakirti: An elder of the City of Vaisali. Although he was a layperson, he was extremely knowledgeable about the doctrines

北、上、下；意指每一處。

十善：不殺生、不偷盜、不邪淫、不妄語、不兩舌、不惡口、不綺語、不貪欲、不瞋恚、不愚癡。

藥師如來：東方琉璃世界的教主，以其十二大願的願力成就佛道。

三大阿僧祇劫：劫是古印度衡量時間的單位，代表極大時限之時間單位。佛教沿用，以劫作為基礎，來說明世界生成與毀滅之過程。三大阿僧祇劫代表菩薩發心到成佛的時間。

三毒：指貪、瞋、癡。

三學：戒、定、慧。

三寶：佛、法、僧。

維摩居士：毘舍離城之長者。雖在俗塵，然精通大乘佛

of Mahayana Buddhism, and was highly cultivated.

Xuanzang: (602-664 C.E.), a great master in the Chinese Tang Dynasty. He is one of four great translators of texts in Buddhist history. He studied in India for seventeen years and was responsible for bringing many collections of works, images, and pictures, as well as one-hundred and fifty relics to China from India. His famous work is entitled *Buddhist Records of the Western Regions*.

教教義，且修為高遠。

玄奘：西元602至664年，唐朝高僧。他為四大譯經僧之一。他曾留學印度十七年，從印度帶回許多經典、佛像，及一百五十顆舍利。他著名的書為「大唐西域記」。

English Publications by Venerable Master Hsing Yun

Buddha's Light Publishing:

1. Between Ignorance and Enlightenment (I)
2. Between Ignorance and Enlightenment (II)
3. Between Ignorance and Enlightenment (III)
   - A Moment, A Lifetime
4. Between Ignorance and Enlightenment (IV)
   - A Life of Pulses and Minuses
5. Between Ignorance and Enlightenment (V)
   - Let Go, Move on
6. The Awakening Life
7. Fo Guang Study
8. Sutra of the Medicine Buddha
   - with an Introduction, Comments and Prayer
9. From the Four Noble Truths to the Four Universal Vows
   - An Integration of the Mahayana and Theravada Schools
10. On Buddhist Democracy, Freedom and Equality
11. Of Benefit to Oneself and Others
    - A Critique of the Six Perfections
12. Pearls of Wisdom
    - Prayers for Engaged Living (I)
13. Pearls of Wisdom
    - Prayers for Engaged Living (II)
14. Humanistic Buddhism - a Blueprint for Life
15. Venerable Master Hsing Yun - Star and Cloud
    - Buddhist Legends of Adventure and Courage

Wisdom Publications:

16. Only a Great Rain
    - A Guide to Chinese Buddhist Meditation
17. Describing the Indescribable
    - A Commentary on the Diamond Sutra

Weatherhill, Inc.:

18. Being Good
    - Buddhist Ethics for Everyday Life
19. Lotus in a Stream

- Basic Buddhism for Beginners

iUniverse.com, Inc.:
20. Humble Table, Wise Fare
    - Gifts for Life

Peter Lang Publishing:
21. The Lions Roar
    - Actualizing Buddhism in Daily Life and Building the Pure Land in Our Midst

Hsi Lai University Press:
22. Handing Down the Light
23. Perfectly Willing
24. Happily Ever After
25. How I Practice Humanistic Buddhism
26. Where is Your Buddha Nature
27. The Carefree Life
28. Humble Table, Wise Fare
    - Hospitality for the Heart (I)
29. Humble Table, Wise Fare
    - Hospitality for the Heart (I)
30. Cloud and Water
    - An Interpretation of Chan Poems
31. Contemporary Thoughts on Humanistic Buddhism
32. Keeping Busy is the Best Nourishment

Spanish Publications by Venerable Master Hsing Yun
1. La Esencia Del Budismo
2. Charlas Sobre Ch'an

Portuguese Publications by Venerable Master Hsing Yun
1. Cultivando O Bem
2. Hist'orias Ch'an
3. Espalhando